Men-at-Arms • 454

The Seminole Wars 1818–58

Ron Field • Illustrated by Richard Hook

Series editor Martin Windrow

First published in Great Britain in 2009 by Osprey Publishing,
Midland House, West Way, Botley, Oxford OX2 0PH, UK
443 Park Avenue South, New York, NY 10016, USA

Email: info@ospreypublishing.com

ISBN: 978 1 84603 461 9
e-book ISBN: 978 1 84908 097 2

Editor: Martin Windrow
Design: Melissa Orrom Swan, Oxford
Index by Michael Forder
Originated by United Graphic Pte Ltd
Printed in China through World Print Ltd.

09 10 11 12 13 10 9 8 7 6 5 4 3 2 1

A CIP catalog record for this book is available from the British Library

FOR A CATALOGUE OF ALL BOOKS PUBLISHED BY OSPREY MILITARY
AND AVIATION PLEASE CONTACT:

Osprey Direct, c/o Random House Distribution Center,
400 Hahn Road, Westminster, MD 21157
E-mail: uscustomerservice@ospreypublishing.com

Osprey Direct, The Book Service Ltd, Distribution Centre,
Colchester Road, Frating Green, Colchester, Essex, CO7 7DW
E-mail: customerservice@ospreypublishing.com

Osprey Publishing is supporting the Woodland Trust, the UK's leading
Woodland conservation charity, by funding the dedication of trees.

www.ospreypublishing.com

Author's acknowledgements

My thanks go to Alan Thrower, William T. Cooper, William J. Schultz, MD,
David Sullivan, Charles H. Cureton and Don Troiani for their kind assistance
in the preparation of this title.

Artist's Note

Readers may care to note that the original paintings from which the color
plates in this book were prepared are available for private sale. All reproduction
copyright whatsoever is retained by the Publishers. All enquiries should be
addressed to:

Richard Hook,
PO Box 475, Hailsham, E.Sussex BN27 2SL, UK

The Publishers regret that they can enter into no correspondence upon
this matter.

OPPOSITE **Yahahajo, or Mad Wolf, was the second principal
war chief of the Seminole nation, and was selected by
the council to inspect the western lands assigned to the
Seminole during the meeting at Payne's Landing in 1832.
He reported favorably, and was one of the 16 chiefs who
signed the treaty the following year. Later wavering
between the pro- and anti-American Seminole factions,
he finally joined the latter under Micanopy, and fought
against selling any land to the USA. He was killed by
a dragoon patrol on the banks of the Ocklewahah River.
He is depicted here wearing a turban of red-spotted blue
trade cloth with a silver band and red ostrich plume, and
a "long shirt" of black or very dark blue with red stripes.
Note the "peace medal." (Author's collection)**

THE SEMINOLE WARS 1818–58

INTRODUCTION

After six years of preliminary skirmishing, between the years 1818 and 1858 the United States fought three wars with the Seminoles and their allies. At issue were the lands inhabited by these Native Americans and by the blacks, both free and slave, who lived under their protection in Florida.

Many Creek (Muskogee) communities were forced east and south out of Georgia and Alabama during the early years of American independence. The Seminoles evolved from various Lower Creek tribes from Georgia who moved into Spanish Florida, joined early in the 19th century by larger numbers of Upper Creeks from Alabama. The two peoples spoke separate languages; the name "Seminole," derived from the Creek word *simanóoli* meaning "runaway," was used from about 1775. These immigrants mixed with remnants of the destroyed Apalachee tribe of northern Florida, other tribal groups, and sizeable numbers of African runaways, to form the Seminole confederation. By the early 19th century the Seminole people had adopted many of the features found in white frontier society. They lived in cabins, herded cattle, rotated their crops, and actively conducted trade with Great Britain, Spain and the USA. By the beginning of the century firearms were rapidly replacing bows and arrows for hunting game, and metal pots and pans were beginning to take the place of traditional pottery and reed baskets.

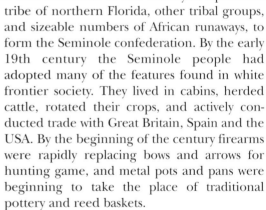

Inhabiting Spanish colonial territory, during the War of 1812 the Seminoles sided with the British. Americans objected to the Spanish protection and clandestine British support given to the Floridian Native Americans thereafter, and to the presence in their communities of blacks living both as free men and as slaves, and the US government eventually decided to take action. This resulted in three periods of bitter warfare spread over 40 years, culminating in the final removal west of virtually all the Seminoles by 1858.

Although the second and longest Seminole War would involve perhaps 40,000 American troops during seven years, the Florida

The Seminole peoples were successful hunters, fishermen and farmers of largely Creek (Muskogee) origin, who lived peacefully in settlements throughout Florida prior to European encroachment. They were later joined by Africans escaping from slavery in the Carolinas and Georgia, who became their close allies in the three bloody wars fought against invaders in defence of their homeland. Originally published in *Vues et Souvenirs de l'Amerique du Nord* by Francis Comte de Castelnau in 1842, this drawing depicts a Lower Creek village on the Apalachicola River. (Florida Photographic Collection)

MajGen Andrew Jackson was ordered to lead the campaign against the Seminoles in December 1817. He conducted a series of decisive actions which resulted in the capture of the Spanish forts at St Marks and Pensacola. This led to the Spanish decision to cede Florida to the United States by the Adams–Onís Treaty on February 22, 1819. In 1821, Jackson was named military governor of Florida Territory. (*Pictorial Life of Jackson*, 1847)

campaigns would usually involve only modest numbers at any one time, and the cost in battle casualties was low. However, deaths from sickness were significant, and these campaigns – fought in the twilight of thick woodlands and swamps among a bewildering maze of waterways – were always an exhausting ordeal for the US regulars and volunteers committed to them, especially in the tropical heat of summer. They were characterized by the extreme difficulties of cross-country movement and of supplying troops in the wilderness, and by the frustrations of trying to locate and bring to battle groups of only a few score or a few hundred Native Americans who were masters of their terrain and who employed the tactics of evasion and ambush to fight at times and places of their own choosing. In the end, American victory was achieved by a combination of the destruction of the Seminoles' agricultural resources, and simple bribery.

* * *

The first major act of aggression leading to the First Seminole War occurred in the spring of 1812, when President James Madison backed a plan to take possession of Spanish East Florida. War with Great Britain was imminent, and the United States government – anxious lest this territory be occupied by British landing forces – requested permission for an American occupation. When the Spanish authorities refused, BrigGen George Mathews of the Georgia militia was appointed to command the invasion force of 220 men, described by those critical of the action as consisting of "a few malcontents" plus "men of desperate fortunes from Georgia." Seizing Amelia Island, on the Atlantic coast adjacent to the border between Georgia and Florida, as a base of operations, and backed by several US Navy gunboats anchored nearby, Mathews promptly received the surrender of the Spanish garrison at Fernandina.

With the ranks of his tiny invasion force soon swelled to about 800, Mathews next besieged St Augustine, about 50 miles down the coast. However, Congress became alarmed at the possibility of outright war with Spain at the same time as the coming war against Britain (the two nations were then allies in the Peninsular War against Napoleon's France), and Mathews was replaced on April 12, 1812 by David Mitchell, Governor of Georgia. However, Mitchell made no change in policy, and before the end of 1812 the US had annexed what was named the Mobile District of West Florida to the Mississippi Territory.

The war with Britain lasted from June 1812 until December 1814 on paper and until February 1815 in practice, and during its final campaign British troops landed at Pensacola. They encouraged Seminole raiding parties, including runaway black slaves, to harry American settlements, farms and plantations, and this intermittent conflict along the Georgia border continued long after the official cessation of hostilities. Distracted by Creole revolutions elsewhere in her American colonies, Spain could not garrison what remained of her Florida possessions with enough troops to control the border, and Spanish impotence soon exhausted the patience of BrigGen Edmund P. Gaines, the commander of US forces on the frontier.

During the summer of 1816, Gaines ordered a punitive expedition consisting of elements of the 4th and 7th US Infantry into Florida to attack and destroy the "Negro Fort," an earthen redoubt on the banks of the Apalachicola river. Originally built by the British, this was now occupied by a garrison of escaped slaves (called "the Exiles" by the whites) and Seminole warriors. The campaign culminated in an attack during which a well-aimed heated shot from Navy gun-vessel No.154 exploded the main powder magazine within the fort, destroying much of the structure and killing about 330 of its defenders. Angered by these events, the Seminoles increased their attacks. Under orders from Gaines, Maj David E. Twiggs, 7th US Infantry, and 250 soldiers launched an assault on Foultown, a Seminole settlement just within American territory, on November 21, 1817. Seminoles under their chief Hornotlimed retaliated nine days later, ambushing and killing all but seven of a boatload of US soldiers and camp followers on the Apalachicola river near Fort Scott.

As revenge for the destruction of his settlement at Foultown, on November 30, 1817 the Seminole leader Hornotlimed and his band ambushed a boat filled with regular soldiers escorting women and children to the safety of Fort Scott. Only six soldiers managed to escape and one woman was taken prisoner. This impression of the event is a fitting visual metaphor for the American troops' experience of all three Seminole Wars: the action is confined to the bottom corner of the engraving, dominated and almost hidden by the oppressive swampland vegetation.
(*Pictorial Life of Jackson*, 1847)

THE FIRST SEMINOLE WAR, 1818–19

Perturbed by the increased violence, the US War Department dispatched MajGen Andrew Jackson to take charge in southern Georgia.

With little respect for the Native American, and even less for diplomatic niceties, Jackson assembled at Nashville a small force of about 500 regular soldiers of the 4th Infantry commanded by Col William King and the 7th Infantry under Col David Brearley. Also in support were about 1,000 militiamen from Georgia, Kentucky, and Tennessee; the latter included elements of the 1st and 2nd Regiments of Tennessee Mounted Gunmen, under Cols R.H. Dyer and Thomas Williamson, and Jackson also had the aid of 2,000 friendly Creek warriors under William McIntosh. At the end of March 1818, after relieving the surrounded garrison of Fort Scott on the Georgia–Florida border, Jackson launched what became known as the First Seminole War by invading Florida.

As the Seminoles retreated before the American advance, Jackson conducted a rapid, two-month campaign of marches, skirmishes and pursuits highlighted by the capture of the Spanish posts of St Marks, on April 5, and Pensacola on May 24, 1818. The former post, situated in Apalachee Bay by the river of the same name, was fortified with 20 pieces of heavy ordnance mounted in well-constructed earthworks; however, the 50-man Spanish garrison offered no resistance, and soon afterwards embarked for Pensacola. Meanwhile, the Seminoles and their black allies concentrated their forces in a stronghold at Suwanee, described by Joshua Giddings as being surrounded by swamps and approachable "only through narrow defiles, which rendered it difficult for an army to reach." While the right wing of Jackson's army faltered during the attack, his left wing made a successful charge and the Seminoles gave way and fell back. Suwanee was captured, and the Native Americans and their black allies dispersed into the swampland.

During this campaign Jackson's forces also captured Josiah Francis and Homathlemico, two Seminole chiefs, and Alexander Arbuthnot and Robert C. Ambrister, two British subjects. The Seminole leaders were lured aboard a US Navy gunboat flying a British flag in the St Marks River, and summarily "tried" and hanged; the two British prisoners were also executed for aiding the Seminoles. These two executions triggered a short-lived protest from the British government and an investigation by Congress. Congressional reports found fault with Jackson's handling of the trial and execution of the two British subjects, but Congress chose not to censure him due to his great popularity. Although the Spanish

Two British subjects, Alexander Arbuthnot and Robert C. Ambrister, were captured by Jackson's forces, and subsequently tried by a military court on charges of aiding the Seminoles and their black allies against the USA. Despite the highly dubious legal basis of any such charges they were executed on April 29, 1818, causing a fierce but short-lived diplomatic dispute with Britain. (*Pictorial Life of Jackson*, 1847)

monarchy strenuously protested Jackson's violation of Spanish colonial territory, the invasion was a clear indication that the Americans could seize Florida whenever they wished. Bowing to the inevitable, and desirous of ridding herself of a profitless possession, on February 22, 1819, Spain ceded Florida to the USA under the Adams–Onís (or Transcontinental) Treaty. The Seminoles now steeled themselves for a full-scale American onslaught at some point in the future.

* * *

In 1823 the US government negotiated the Treaty of Moultrie Creek with the Seminoles; this established a reservation for them in central Florida, but six chiefs were allowed to keep their villages along the Apalachicola River. Although the Seminoles settled into the reservation there were isolated clashes with Americans, and Fort King was built close to the reservation agency (near present-day Ocala) to police the area. Peace lasted for five years, during which time there were repeated calls for the Seminoles to be sent to the Indian Territory (Oklahoma) west of the Mississippi. In 1826 a Seminole delegation including Tukosee Mathla, Neamathla and the black leader Abraham went to Washington, DC, to ask of President John Quincy Adams that the Big Swamp area be added to the reservation in Central Florida.

Meanwhile, the status of runaway slaves was a continuing

Also known as the "White Warrior," William McIntosh was the son of Capt William McIntosh of Savannah, Georgia, who was sent into the Creek nation to recruit them to fight for the British during the Revolutionary War. As leader of the friendly Creeks, he fought against the Seminoles alongside Andrew Jackson's forces in the First Seminole War. In 1825 he signed the Treaty of Indian Springs, giving Georgia large tracts of Creek land; he was killed by Etomie Tustennuggee, another Creek chief, the same year. The essential similarity between Creek and Seminole costume is evident here – see Plate B3. (Author's collection)

Massacre of the Whites by the Indians and Blacks in Florida.

Published in 1836 by D.F. Blanchard, this engraving depicts the slaughter of white settlers in Florida at the beginning of the Second Seminole War, and is one of the only known images of the period showing blacks and Native Americans fighting as allies. (*An Authentic Narrative of the Seminole War*, 1836)

irritation between Seminoles and whites, since new plantations established in Florida led to an increase in the number of slaves who could run away to join the Native Americans. Worried about the possibility of an Indian uprising and/or a slave insurrection, Governor William P. DuVal requested additional US troops for Florida. Instead, Fort King was closed in 1828. Running short of food and finding local hunting poor, many Seminoles started wandering off the reservation. Furthermore, their old enemy Andrew Jackson was elected President of the United States that same year. As a result, in 1830 Congress passed the Indian Removal Act, which was designed to move all Native Americans west of the Mississippi.

During the spring of 1832 the Seminoles on the reservation were summoned to a meeting at Payne's Landing on the Oklawaha River, where a treaty was agreed whereby a delegation of seven chiefs would inspect land on the Creek reservation in Arkansas Territory and, if they found it suitable, they would agree to removal west. After inspection of the reservation in March 1833 the US government claimed the Seminole leaders had signed an agreement to move, while many other Seminoles denied knowledge of any such agreement. The majority objected vehemently to relocation, since they could not co-exist with the Creeks as neighbors. However, some of those living in the villages in the area of the Apalachicola River did agree to be moved, and went west in 1834.

The US Senate finally ratified the Treaty of Payne's Landing in April 1834, which gave the Seminoles three years to move west of the Mississippi. Assuming the starting point to have been 1832, the Americans expected the Seminoles to be gone by 1835. Fort King was reopened in 1834 and a new agent named Wiley Thompson was appointed. He summoned the chiefs together at the fort in October of that year to persuade them to move; when they told him that they had no intention of moving, Thompson requested reinforcements for Fort King and Fort Brooke. General Duncan L. Clinch also warned Washington that the Seminoles did not intend to move and that more troops would be needed.

In March 1835 Thompson informed the Seminole chiefs that if they did not leave they would be removed by force. Some of the Indian leaders agreed to go west, while others, including Micanopy and Osceola, responded with delaying tactics. Recognizing that many of the

Seminoles were going to resist forced displacement, Florida began to prepare for war. Seminole war parties began raiding farms and settlements, and families fled to forts, large townships, or out of the territory altogether. A militia supply train was captured by Osceola, and sugar plantations along the Atlantic coast south of St Augustine were destroyed, with many of the plantation slaves joining forces with the Seminoles.

THE SECOND SEMINOLE WAR, 1835–42

The "Dade massacre," 1835

Only 11 companies of US regulars, amounting to about 550 soldiers, were stationed in Florida by 1835. One company was stationed at Fort King, at risk of being cut off, while three garrisoned Fort Brooke on the east bank of the Hillsborough River in present-day Tampa. With news that reinforcements were on the way, two of the companies at Fort Brooke were ordered to march to the relief of Fort King. This column was commanded by Brevet Maj Francis L. Dade, 4th Infantry, and totaled 110 men, comprising one company of the 3rd Infantry and a detachment of the 2nd Artillery with a 6-pdr gun. The little force set out on December 23, 1835, but was shadowed by the Seminoles led by chiefs Micanopy and Jumper. Five days later it was ambushed. The possibility of attack seems to have been remote in the soldiers' minds, since they were wearing their overcoats over their cartridge boxes to protect them from the winter weather. As a result they had difficulty getting at their cartridges on receiving the first fire from the Seminoles, and took heavy casualties. According to an eyewitness account by Seminole leader Halpatter Tustenuggee (known to the whites as "Alligator"):

> Jumper gave the whoop, Micanopy fired the first rifle, the signal agreed upon, when every Indian arose and fired, which laid upon the ground, dead, more than half the white men. The cannon was discharged several times, but the men who loaded it were shot down as soon as the smoke cleared away ... As we were returning to the swamp supposing all were dead, an Indian came up and said the white men were building a fort of logs. Jumper and myself, with ten warriors, returned. As we approached, we saw six men behind two logs placed one above another, with the cannon a short distance off ... We soon came near, as the balls went over us. They had guns, but no powder, we looked in the [cartridge] boxes afterwards and found they were empty.

Originally published in 1842, this engraving depicts the defeat of troops under Maj Francis L. Dade, 4th US Infantry, on December 28, 1835. Survivors of the initial attack attempted in vain to defend themselves behind a small triangular breastwork before being overrun and killed by Seminoles led by Halpatter Tustenuggee. (*Indian Wars of the United States*, 1852)

While marching to Fort King the column led by Gen Edmund P. Gaines discovered the bodies of Dade's command. The full dress uniforms shown in this engraving are inaccurate for the period – and so, of course, are the clean-picked skeletons: the corpses were only six weeks old, and an eyewitness mentioned their uniforms. (Author's collection)

Of the three men who survived the massacre, Edwin De Courcey was hunted down and killed by a Seminole the next day, while the other two survivors, Ransome Clarke and Joseph Sprague, returned to Fort Brooke. Taking refuge underwater in a nearby pond, Sprague saw nothing of the battle; but before dying of his wounds, Clarke gave a graphic account of how the Seminole were initially driven back by the cannon, but eventually overran the small triangular breastwork hastily erected by the remainder of Dade's desperate command.

On December 29, 1835, Gen Clinch marched out of Fort Drane, about 20 miles northwest of Fort King, intent on attacking a Seminole stronghold on the Withlacoochee River. He had 200 regulars consisting of detachments from the 1st, 2nd and 3rd Artillery, plus about 550 Floridian volunteers whose term of service was due to expire on January 1, 1836. When this force reached the river they could not find the ford, and Clinch ordered his regular troops ferried across as an advance guard. Once across and relaxing, the soldiers were attacked and only saved themselves by fixing bayonets and charging the Seminoles, at the cost of four dead and 59 wounded. The militia provided covering fire as the remaining regulars withdrew back across the river.

Gaines' campaign, 1836

News of the Dade massacre and the failure of the Clinch expedition sent shockwaves through Washington, DC, and the reaction was swift. MajGen Winfield Scott was placed in charge of the war and Congress appropriated $620,000 to pay for it. Volunteer companies were enlisted in Georgia, Alabama and South Carolina to reinforce the small regular US Army, which at that date only had about 7,500 men. Commanding the Western Military Department, BrigGen Gaines gathered together a force of about 1,100 men in New Orleans; these consisted of a regiment of Louisiana volunteers under Col Persifer F. Smith and some regulars of the 4th Infantry. A lack of logistic preparation would dominate Gaines' expedition; he sailed his troops to Fort Brooke, but when he arrived he found its garrison low on supplies. Under the belief that Scott had sent supplies to Fort King, Gaines marched his men on to that post. En route they found the site of the Dade massacre, and buried the bodies in three mass graves. Gaines' command reached Fort King after a nine-day march, only to find that its garrison, too, was very short of supplies.

Finally receiving seven days' worth of rations from Gen Clinch at Fort Drane, Gaines led his men back to Fort Brooke by a different route, with the intention of engaging the Seminoles in their stronghold called the Cove of the Withlacoochee River. Without reliable maps or dependable scouts, he reached the same location where Clinch had been defeated six weeks earlier, and failed to cross the river. With insufficient rations to return to Fort King, Gaines sent word to Clinch for help, and ordered his command to construct a fortification called Camp Izard (after Lt James F. Izard, Regiment of Dragoons, who was mortally wounded attempting to cross the Withlacoochee.) It was hoped that the Seminoles would concentrate around Camp Izard and that troops under Clinch could mount a surprise attack and crush them between the two forces; however, Gen Scott ordered Clinch to remain at Fort Drane. Besieged for eight days, Gaines' men were reduced to eating horses and mules. Despite a further directive to remain at his post, Clinch disobeyed orders and marched for Camp Izard just one day before the arrival of Scott's permission to do so. He finally reached the beleaguered post on March 6, 1836, chasing away the Seminoles.

This engraving by Felix Darley shows Seminoles attacking a stage coach in Georgia during the spring of 1836. (*Our Country*, 1905)

Scott's campaign, 1836

After the failure of this ill-prepared expedition Gen Scott assembled men and supplies for a grand campaign against the Seminoles. Totaling 5,000 men, three columns were to converge on the Cove of the Withlacoochee. One column, under the command of BrigGen Clinch accompanied by Scott himself, would move south from Fort Drane; a second under BrigGen Abraham Eustis would march southwest from Volusia on the St Johns River; and a third, led by Col William Lindsay, would move north from Fort Brooke. The plan was for the three columns to arrive at the Cove simultaneously so as to prevent the Seminoles from escaping.

In the event, all three columns were delayed. Eustis was two days late leaving Volusia because of an attack by Seminoles. Clinch and Lindsay only reached their positions on March 28 and, marching through uncharted territory, the column led by Eustis did not arrive until two days later. Meanwhile, Clinch crossed the river on March 29 to attack the Seminoles, but found the villages in the Cove deserted. Although Eustis did engage in a skirmish en route, and burned the village of black Seminole leader Abraham, the whole operation had killed or captured only a handful of hostiles. By March 31 all three commanders were running low on supplies, and headed for Fort Brooke. The failure of Scott's expedition to effectively engage the Seminoles was regarded as a defeat, and was blamed on insufficient planning and the difficulties of the climate and terrain.

Call's campaign, 1836

Following this second failed attempt to find them, fix them and bring them to battle, the Seminoles launched attacks on posts across Florida. In June a blockhouse on the Withlacoochee River was besieged, and the garrison was only rescued after 48 days. On July 23 the Cape Florida lighthouse was attacked and burned (it would not be repaired until 1846). The Army was also suffering terribly from disease, and Fort Drane was abandoned in July with five out of seven officers and 140 men on the sick list. The war promised to be long and expensive; Congress appropriated another $1.5 million, and allowed volunteers to enlist for up to a year.

MajGen Winfield Scott was given command of operations in Florida at the beginning of 1836, but by March of that year his campaign to destroy the Seminole stronghold at the Cove of the Withlacoochee had failed. (Florida State Archives RC12182)

Richard Keith Call, who had commanded the Florida volunteers when Clinch marched on the Cove of the Withlacoochee in December 1835, was appointed Governor of the Territory of Florida on March 16, 1836. He proposed a summer campaign using the militia and volunteers instead of the regular army, but, although the War Department agreed to this proposal, delays in preparations postponed the start of operations until the end of September. Call also intended to attack the Cove of the Withlacoochee, and sent most of his supplies down the west coast of the peninsula and up the Withlacoochee River in order to establish a forward supply base. Meanwhile, he marched with the main body of his men to the abandoned Fort Drane, and then on to the Withlacoochee. When he reached it on October 13 he found that the river was in flood and not fordable, and his volunteers could not make rafts for a crossing since they had not brought axes with them. Furthermore, the Seminoles on the opposite bank shot at any soldier who showed himself. Call turned west along the north bank of the river hoping to find his supply depot; however, the steamer bringing the supplies had sunk in the lower part of the Withlacoochee, and what remained was much further downstream than expected. Running out of food, Call led his men back to Fort Drane, admitting the failure of yet another expedition to capture the Cove.

During mid-November 1836, Call tried again with a force of Florida militia and Tennessee volunteers. This time he succeeded in crossing the Withlacoochee, but found the villages of the Cove abandoned. Deploying his men on either bank of the river, he marched south until, on November 17, he encountered and destroyed a large Seminole encampment. The action continued the next day, with the Seminoles retreating towards the Wahoo Swamp. Re-uniting his force, Call entered the swamp on November 21, but his advance was halted by a deep stream.

Major David Moniac (a mixed-blood Creek, who was the first Native American to graduate from West Point) tried to determine the depth of the stream, but was shot and killed in the attempt. Unable to reach the Seminoles and with supplies again running short, Call withdrew and led his men to Volusia. On December 9, 1836, he was relieved of command and replaced by MajGen Thomas Jesup, who led the exhausted volunteers and militia back to Fort Brooke. With the expiry of their terms of enlistment at the end of December, they went home.

Jesup's campaigns, 1837

The US Army had only four major-generals at the commencement of the Second Seminole War, with Alexander Macomb, Jr, as commanding general. Since both Edmund Gaines and Winfield Scott had signally failed to defeat the Seminoles, Thomas Jesup was the last senior officer available to attempt the task. Having just suppressed a Creek uprising in western Georgia and eastern Alabama (the campaign known as the Creek War of 1836), Jesup brought a new approach to the operations in Florida. Rather than sending large columns out to try to force the Seminoles into fighting a set-piece battle, he concentrated on wearing them down with a larger military presence that threatened their families and resources. He eventually had a force of more than 9,000 men under his command, half of which consisted of Army regulars, plus a battalion of Marines consisting of 38 officers and about 400 enlisted men.

Under command of Archibald Henderson, the Marines had marched south from their barracks in Washington, DC, to participate in the Creek War. Legend has it that Henderson nailed a notice to the front door of the Marine Corps headquarters building which declared "Gone to fight the Indians. Will be back when the war is over." Arriving too late to see any action against the Creeks, the Marines spent the remainder of the summer of 1836 patrolling the Georgia/Alabama border both on foot and by steamboat. Ordered further south to join Jesup's forces in September, they took part in a battle with the Seminoles on January 27, 1837 as part of a composite brigade under Henderson which also included Army regulars, Georgia volunteers, and friendly Creeks.

Attacking a Seminole village near the Hatchee-Lustee River, they captured some women and children along with 100 pack ponies and 1,400 head of cattle, but the warriors escaped into the swampland. The mounted Marines continued the pursuit, crossing two streams and wounding a number of Seminoles before they finally lost contact.

Although fighting continued for a further month, the Seminole warriors finally agreed in March 1837 to a truce and removal west, having lost their families and main source of food. By the end of that May many chiefs including Micanopy had surrendered, but two important leaders – Osceola and the aged Arpiucki, also known as Sam Jones – had not come in, and were vehemently opposed to relocation. On June 2, 1837 these chiefs with about 200 followers entered the poorly-guarded holding camp at Fort Brooke and led away the 700 Seminoles who had surrendered; the war was on again. Believing that hostilities were largely over, Jesup had assigned many of the regulars elsewhere, while the militia and volunteers had been released from duty.

Given the Florida command on December 9, 1836, MajGen Thomas Sydney Jesup would eventually have some 9,000 troops, militia and volunteers available to him. During 1837–38 a number of Seminole chiefs were forced to submit after the capture of their families and livestock, but Jesup's results were ultimately indecisive. (Florida Photographic Collection)

Despite the onset of summer and the "sickly season" in Florida, and the financial crisis caused by the Panic of 1837, the US Congress appropriated another $1.6 million to pay for the ongoing hostilities. As sporadic fighting continued during the summer and fall of 1837 several important Seminole chiefs, including Osceola and Coeehájo, were captured after being tricked by a false flag of truce. Imprisoned at Fort Moultrie in Charleston, South Carolina, Osceola was dead within three months.

By the end of 1837 Jesup had a large army assembled in Florida, including volunteers from as far away as Missouri and New York. His plan of campaign was to advance down the peninsula with several columns, pushing the Seminoles ever further south. General Joseph Marion Hernández led a column down the east coast; Gen Eustis took his column along the St Johns River, while Col Zachary Taylor led a column from Fort Brooke into the middle of the state, and then southwards between the Kissimmee and Peace rivers. Meanwhile, a joint Army/Navy force (the "Mosquito Fleet") under Lt Levin Powell, USN, patrolled the lower east coast of Florida, and other troops patrolling from a chain of blockhouses protected the northern part of the territory from Seminole raids.

It was Taylor who saw the first major action. Leaving Fort Gardiner on the upper Kissimmee River with 1,000 men on December 19, 1837, he caught up with about 400 Seminoles led by Halpatter Tustenuggee, Arpiucki, and Coacoochee on the north shore of Lake Okeechobee on Christmas Day. The Seminoles defended a "hammock" (a patch of ground rising above the swamp and waterways, covered with saw-grass). After an attack by the first line of volunteers failed, the regulars and Missouri volunteers forced the Seminoles out of their defensive position, but they managed to escape across the lake. Although only about a dozen Seminoles had been killed, against 26 American dead and 112 wounded, the Battle of Lake Okeechobee was hailed as a great victory.

Taylor next joined the other columns sweeping down the peninsula to pass on the east side of Lake Okeechobee, while the troops along the Caloosahatchee River blocked any passage north on the west side of the lake. Still patrolling the east coast, on January 15, 1838, Lt Powell was

In this Gray & James lithograph Seminoles are shown attacking the blockhouse at Camp Izard near the Withlacoochee River. Forces under Gen Edmund P. Gaines were besieged there for eight days until finally relieved by Gen Clinch on March 6, 1836. (Library of Congress, Prints and Photographs Division, LC-USZ62-11463)

South Carolinian volunteers under Gen Abraham Eustis are shown at a bivouac beside a partially destroyed bridge while probing along the Withlacoochee River in late March or early April 1836. (Library of Congress, Prints and Photographs Division, LC-USZ62-21757)

leading 80 men of the combined Army/Navy force towards a Seminole camp when they found themselves almost completely surrounded by a larger force. After an unsuccessful charge, they fought their way back to their boats at a cost of four dead and 22 wounded. At the end of January, Jesup's marching columns caught up with a large body of Seminoles to the east of Lake Okeechobee. The Seminoles were originally positioned on a hammock, but were driven back across a wide stream, making another stand on the far bank. They eventually disappeared, having caused more casualties than they suffered during what became known as the Battle of Loxahatchee.

Despite these very variable military results, the pressure of the American columns was greatly disrupting the Seminoles' ability to maintain their way of life. As the operations subsided during February 1838 the chiefs Tuskegee and Halleck Hadjo informed Jesup that they would stop fighting if allowed to remain south of Lake Okeechobee. Foreseeing a long and fruitless campaign in the Everglades, the American general favored the idea and wrote to Washington seeking approval. Meanwhile, the Seminole chiefs established a camp near Jesup's army, and the two forces co-existed peacefully. However, Secretary of War Joel Roberts Poinsett rejected the idea and ordered Jesup to continue his campaign. Jesup summoned the chiefs to his camp, but – no doubt mindful of past American treachery – they refused the invitation. Unwilling to allow 500 Seminoles to disappear into the swampland, Jesup sent a force to detain them; they offered very little resistance, possibly realizing that it was futile to continue fighting against such odds.

Taylor's campaign, 1838–39

Requesting permission to be relieved of command in April 1838, Jesup returned to his position as Quartermaster General of the Army, and Zachary Taylor assumed command in Florida. With reduced forces, he concentrated on keeping the Seminoles out of northern Florida in order that settlers could return to their homes. In a continuation of Winfield Scott's tactics, he had 53 new military posts and blockhouses built, and constructed about 848 miles of wagon road by the spring of 1839. However, the Seminoles continued to raid northwards. Meanwhile, in Washington and around the country, support for the war continued to erode due to its length, cost, and indecisive results. As a result, Congress appropriated $5,000 to negotiate a settlement with the Seminoles, and President Martin Van Buren sent MajGen Alexander Macomb to negotiate a new treaty. Initially the Seminoles failed to respond, remembering past broken promises. Eventually Arpiucki sent his chosen successor, Chitto Tustenuggee, to meet with Gen Macomb, and on May 19, 1839, Macomb announced that an agreement had been reached: the Seminoles would stop fighting in exchange for a reservation in southern Florida.

The agreement held for just a few months. A trading post was established on the north shore of the Caloosahatchee River with a detachment of 23 regulars under Col William S. Harney. The Seminoles who visited seemed to be friendly; but on July 23 the post was attacked by a force about ten times its size. A few of the tiny garrison, including Col Harney, were able to reach the river and escaped in boats, but most, along with a number of civilians, were killed at the trading post. The war was on again.

It was not clear who had attacked the trading post. Many blamed a band of mixed Spanish and Native Americans led by Chakaika, while others suspected Arpiucki, who had reached the agreement with Macomb. Anxious to clear his name, Arpiucki promised to turn those responsible for the attack over to Harney within 33 days. Meanwhile, the Seminoles in camp near Fort Lauderdale remained on friendly terms with the soldiers and, on July 27, 1839, officers at the fort were invited to a dance at their camp. Declining the offer, they sent two soldiers and a black interpreter with the gift of a keg of whiskey. The Americans did not have a monopoly on treachery; the soldiers were killed, but the interpreter escaped and returned to the fort to inform the garrison that Arpiucki and Chitto Tustenuggee were involved in the attack. Following these events the fighting spread north once more, and an end to hostilities seemed as far away as ever.

At this point, Taylor attempted to use bloodhounds to hunt down the Seminoles. Although he had received permission to adopt these tactics in 1838 he had not done so. Now he acquired a pack of bloodhounds and handlers

Published in 1848 by James Baillie of New York, this lithograph depicts Zachary Taylor as commander of US forces during the Second Seminole War. On horseback, Taylor presides over a fanciful scene of devastation as infantry with bloodhounds advance on the Seminoles. The use of bloodhounds to hunt for the elusive warriors during 1839 led to a widespread public outcry in the US, and was, in fact, completely ineffective in the Florida wetlands. (Library of Congress LC-USZ62-59036)

from Cuba, courtesy of the territorial government of Florida. Although initial trials of the hounds had mixed results, an outcry arose in the US over fears that the dogs might try to kill or maim the Seminoles, including women and children. Secretary of War Poinsett had to issue an order that the dogs be kept muzzled and leashed while being used for tracking. However, the bloodhounds could not track through water anyway, and the Seminoles easily evaded them.

Armistead's campaigns, 1839–41

In May 1839 Zachary Taylor was granted his request for a transfer, having served longer than any preceding commander in the Second Seminole War. His replacement, BrigGen Walker K. Armistead, had earlier served in Florida as second-in-command to Jesup. Armistead immediately went on the offensive, ordering out 100 soldiers at a time on "search and destroy" missions. For the first time, US forces actively campaigned in Florida during the summer, taking captives and destroying crops and homes. Hidden camps and fields were discovered across central Florida, and by the middle of the summer approximately 500 acres of Seminole crops had been destroyed. This tactic proved very effective, preventing the Seminoles from growing crops to provide food during the winter, and it eventually contributed greatly to their ultimate defeat by 1842.

Armistead made the defense of Florida north of Fort King the responsibility of volunteers and militia, while his regulars worked to confine the Seminoles south of that post. By this time, US regular forces in Florida consisted of the 1st, 2nd, 3rd, 6th, 7th and 8th Infantry, ten companies of the 2nd Dragoons, and nine companies of the 3rd Artillery – the majority of the entire Unites States Army. Meanwhile, at Fort Bankhead on Key Biscayne, Col Harney began training regulars in swamp warfare.

The Navy was also taking a larger role in the war. In late 1839 command of the "Mosquito Fleet" on the east coast passed from Lt Powell to Lt John T. McLaughlin, USN. Based at Tea Table Key in the upper Florida Keys, this force was intended to prevent Cuban and Bahamian traders bringing arms and other supplies to the Seminoles, by placing schooners off shore and barges closer to the mainland. Meanwhile, smaller boats manned by sailors and marines probed up rivers and into the Everglades. An abortive attempt was made to cross the Everglades from west to east in April 1840, but the boats were attacked at the rendezvous point on Cape Sable. McLaughlin did lead a force across the Everglades later that year, however; starting in December 1840, they crossed from east to west in dugout canoes, and were the first white men to make this journey successfully.

In December 1840, Col Harney finally got revenge for his humiliation on the Caloosahatchee River in July 1839. Leading a canoe expedition of 90 men from Fort Dallas into the Everglades along the Miami River, he encountered some Native Americans in canoes and gave chase.

Originally published in 1848, this engraving by N. Orr depicts a detachment of the 2nd Dragoons under Capt B.L. Beall killing a Seminole warrior called Waxehadjo, whose band had recently ambushed a US express rider en route from Fort Cross to Tampa Bay in 1841. After taking refuge underwater, Waxehadjo was gunned down by the dragoons when he finally surfaced for air. His body was then hung from a tree as a warning to others. (*Origin, Progress, and Conclusion of the Florida War*, 1848)

Chief Osceola was the leading opponent of the Treaty of Payne's Landing in 1833, by which a minority of Seminole chiefs signed away their lands in return for a reservation in Indian Territory. Osceola rallied the Seminole bands and fought bitterly against American encroachment during the Second Seminole War. He was finally betrayed and captured in 1837, and taken in chains to South Carolina, where he died at Fort Moultrie in January 1838. He is depicted here wearing a red turban with black and white plumes; a patterned yellow neckerchief; a green "long shirt" with a black pattern and red trim at the cape and skirt; red sash and leggings; a blue-beaded bandolier and belt, and three silver gorgets. See also Plate C1. (Author's collection)

Finding his way to the encampment of a band of mixed-blood Spanish/Native Americans led by Chakaika, his men approached dressed as Seminoles and launched a successful surprise attack. Having killed four and hanged five including Chakaika, with the loss of only one of his own command, Harney received a commendation and a sword from the Legislative Council of Florida, and was subsequently given command of the 2nd Dragoons.

Having received $55,000 from Congress for the purpose of bribing Seminoles to accept resettlement in the west, Gen Armistead managed to convince Coosa Tustenuggee to accepted $5,000 in return for bringing in his band of 60 warriors and their families during the winter of 1840. Lesser chiefs received $200, and every warrior was given $30 and a rifle.

Worth's campaign, 1841–42

During May 1841, Armistead was replaced in command by Col William J. Worth. Due to the unpopularity of the war, which was costing $93,000 per month, Worth was forced to cut back on expenditure. However, continuing the summertime "search and destroy" policy begun by Armistead, he effectively drove most the Seminoles out of their old stronghold in the Cove of the Withlacoochee, and much of the rest of northern Florida. The rest of that year was mainly spent bribing the remaining Seminoles to surrender and accept transportation west. Among these was Coacoochee, or Wild Cat, who was freed after his arrest at Fort Pierce, and bribed with $8,000 by Worth to persuade other Seminoles to surrender; as a result, 211 turned themselves in, including most of his band.

As the number of Native Americans in Florida decreased it became easier for those left behind to stay hidden. Early in 1842 Worth recommended that the remaining Seminoles be left in peace if they remained in southern Florida, and eventually he did receive authorization to allow them to establish an informal reservation in the southwest of the territory. He also received permission to declare an end to the war on a date of his choosing. Seminole bands remaining in Florida included those led by Holata Mico, or Bolek, from which was derived his nickname "Billy Bowlegs;" Arpiucki; Chipco; and the black Seminole leader Thlocklo Tustenuggee or "Tiger-Tail."

In August 1842 the US Congress passed the Armed Occupation Act, which provided free land to white settlers who improved it and were prepared to defend it against Native Americans. A total of 1,317 grants totaling 210,720 acres were registered in 1842 and 1843. In the same month, Worth met with the chiefs still in Florida, and each warrior was offered a rifle, money and one year's worth of rations in return for agreeing to move west. Although some accepted the offer, most hoped

Published in 1878, this lithograph by John Reuben Chapin inaccurately shows American forces under Zachary Taylor fighting the Seminoles at Lake Okeechobee on Christmas Day, 1837, as wearing 1850s uniforms. Although this action was hailed as a great US victory most of the Seminoles managed to escape. (*Battles of America by Sea and Land*, 1878)

eventually to move to the reservation in southwestern Florida. Believing that the remaining Native Americans in Florida would either go west or move to the reservation, Worth declared the war to be at an end on August 14, 1842.

Although sporadic fighting dragged on as Tiger-Tail and Otiarche continued to resist reservation life, Worth reported in April 1843 that only about 300 Native Americans remained in Florida, all living on the reservation and no longer posing any threat to white settlement. In fact, chiefs such as Halleck Tustenuggee, Jumper, and the black Seminole leaders Abraham and John Horse had once again retreated into the Everglades and were determined to continue their resistance to white encroachment.

The Second Seminole War cost approximately $40 million. A total of more than 40,000 regular soldiers, militia and volunteers served in the war at one time or another. Some 300 US Army, Navy and Marine Corps personnel were killed in action, along with 55 volunteers, and a further 1,145 regulars and volunteers died of disease. There is no record of the number of Seminoles killed in action. A great many died of disease or starvation, either in Florida or on the journey west, and many others after they reached Indian Territory.

Col William J. Worth, 8th US Infantry, took command of US forces in Florida after defeating the Seminoles at Palaldaklaha on April 19, 1842. Continuing the "search and destroy" tactics begun by Gen Walker K. Armistead, he was able to declare the Second Seminole War over by August of that year. He achieved the rank of brevet major-general following further service in the Mexican War of 1846–48. (USAMHI/photo by Jim Enos)

* * *

Calm prevailed for a while following the end of the Second Seminole War, but when Florida achieved statehood in 1845 efforts resumed to relocate all remaining Seminoles west to Indian Territory. During the next four years sporadic skirmishing kept tempers inflamed. When a small band of Seminoles killed a white fisherman on the Indian River near the lower east coast in January 1849, the Florida legislature panicked and requested help from the Federal government to avert a full-scale Native American uprising. By the end of 1850, BrigGen David E. Twiggs had about 1,700 regular troops in the state. Once again, bribes were offered in an attempt to entice the Seminoles west, but only 85 agreed to leave their homes. Others, including Billy Bowlegs, refused to comply.

In 1851, Gen Luther Blake was appointed by Secretary of the Interior Alexander H. Stuart to move the remaining Seminoles west. Blake had successfully driven the Cherokee from Georgia, and was thought capable of removing the Seminoles from Florida. To this end he was granted

funds sufficient to pay $800 to every adult male who agreed to leave, and every woman and child $450. By July 1852 he had arranged for just 16 Seminoles to be sent to Indian Territory, but Billy Bowlegs and several other chiefs remained difficult to persuade. Finally extracting a promise from them to leave their homeland in 1852, he took the Seminole leaders to Washington, DC, where they signed an agreement and President Millard Fillmore presented Bowlegs with a peace medal. On this occasion the Seminole chief was described in the *Illustrated London News* as being "utterly surprised at what he has seen … and is perfectly satisfied that, with the big guns, powerful steam-boats, and 'much folks' which he finds, the great Seminole nation itself must yield before the white man." The Seminole delegation was then taken on a tour that included Baltimore, Philadelphia and New York City – but on their return to Florida the chiefs repudiated the Washington agreement.

THE THIRD SEMINOLE WAR, 1855–58

Settlers and Seminoles continued to skirmish. On December 19, 1855, Lt George K. Hartsuff, 2nd Artillery, and a small surveying party from Fort Myers discovered that Fort Shackleton, a partially-built post in the Big Cypress Swamp, had been burned. In retaliation Hartsuff's party destroyed a Seminole banana plantation near the camp of Billy Bowlegs. The following morning 35 Seminole warriors led by Bowlegs attacked Hartsuff's encampment, killing two men and wounding four, including Hartsuff. According to Andrew P. Canova, who served as a volunteer in the Third Seminole War:

> Hartsoff [sic] ran into the water, but began emptying his Colt's revolver at the Indians, who were soon dismayed by the strange weapon, which did not seem to require loading, but which seemed to them to be able to kill every one of them, while they were loading their rifles. It was the first revolver they had seen, and Bowlegs promised to cease firing if Hartsoff would come out and show his pistol. This ruse did not succeed, and the Indians retreated.

Meanwhile one of the other wounded men managed to escape back to Fort Myers, and a company of infantry marched to the rescue, finding Hartsuff and others still alive but in a critical condition.

When the news of the attack reached Tampa, militia companies were hastily assembled in order to man the forts along the Peace River valley. Governor James Broome began to organize units of Florida Mounted Volunteers, three of which were armed, equipped and paid by the Federal government to supplement the lack of regulars in Florida – these had dwindled to a mere 871 by 1855. Broome also kept another 400 men mobilized under state control, half of whom conducted mounted patrols while the remainder tended crops. General Jesse Carter was appointed by Governor Broome as "special agent … without military rank" to lead the state troops.

These volunteers provided only an imperfect defense against Seminole raiders during 1856, and although the cost in lives was tiny the raids caused widespread unease. On January 6, two men were killed south of the Miami River, which caused the settlers in the area to flee for

A fierce Seminole warrior, Thlocko Tustenuggee, also known as Tiger-Tail, fought in the battle of the Wahoo Swamp on November 26, 1836, where he was wounded in the left hand. Finally captured towards the end of 1842, he died while imprisoned at the New Orleans Barracks in January 1843. (*Origin, Progress, and Conclusion of the Florida War*, 1848)

safety to Fort Dallas and Key Biscayne. In March, about 20 Seminoles under Ocsen Tustenuggee attacked a wood-cutting party outside Fort Denaud, killing five of the six men. The Seminoles also raided along the coast south of Tampa Bay, killing one man and burning a house in present-day Sarasota. They also tried to attack "Braden Castle," the plantation home of Dr Joseph Braden, in what is now Bradenton. Although the defenses there were too strong, they led away seven slaves and three mules. In this instance the militia caught up with the Seminoles; they killed and scalped two and recaptured the slaves.

Harney's campaign, 1856–57

In September 1856, BrigGen William S. Harney returned to Florida as commander of Federal troops. Under his command were the 5th Infantry, four companies of the 1st Artillery, three companies of the 3rd Artillery, and ten companies of the 4th Artillery; these 2,200 men represented almost 13 per cent of the entire regular US Army at that time. Harney was also authorized to call on Governor Broome for about ten additional companies of mounted volunteers. Quartermaster General Jesup also provided 33 18ft-long shallow draft boats for use in the Florida marshlands. Reviving the tactics employed during the Second Seminole War, Harney set up a chain of outposts across central Florida, and patrols probed deep into Seminole territory. He planned to confine the Seminoles to the Big Cypress Swamp and the Everglades, believing that they would be unable to survive there during the wet season. In so doing, he hoped to catch them when they left their flooded sanctuaries seeking dry land for raising crops.

Harney was also advised by Secretary of War (and future Confederate President) Jefferson Davis that each Seminole who surrendered would receive the Federal bounty offered for his or her capture. The hope was that they would be more likely to surrender given the fact that on August 7, 1857, one of their original objections to going west had presumably been removed, when they were promised a reservation separate from their old enemies the Creeks, plus $250,000 annuity. Thus, before com-

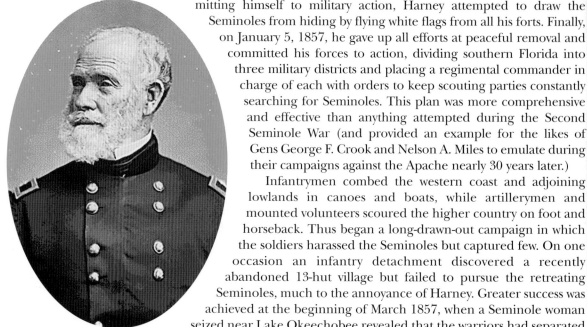

Having served with distinction during the Second Seminole War, Gen William S. Harney was appointed to command troops in the final conflict in Florida during September 1856. His "search and destroy" tactics did much to wear down the remaining Seminoles before his transfer west in April 1857. (US National Archives NWDNS-111-B-4693)

mitting himself to military action, Harney attempted to draw the Seminoles from hiding by flying white flags from all his forts. Finally, on January 5, 1857, he gave up all efforts at peaceful removal and committed his forces to action, dividing southern Florida into three military districts and placing a regimental commander in charge of each with orders to keep scouting parties constantly searching for Seminoles. This plan was more comprehensive and effective than anything attempted during the Second Seminole War (and provided an example for the likes of Gens George F. Crook and Nelson A. Miles to emulate during their campaigns against the Apache nearly 30 years later.)

Infantrymen combed the western coast and adjoining lowlands in canoes and boats, while artillerymen and mounted volunteers scoured the higher country on foot and horseback. Thus began a long-drawn-out campaign in which the soldiers harassed the Seminoles but captured few. On one occasion an infantry detachment discovered a recently abandoned 13-hut village but failed to pursue the retreating Seminoles, much to the annoyance of Harney. Greater success was achieved at the beginning of March 1857, when a Seminole woman seized near Lake Okeechobee revealed that the warriors had separated into small parties, vowing to die fighting rather than leave Florida. She also stated that the aged Chief Arpiucki was somewhere in the Big Cypress Swamp. Harney was also encouraged by news that detachments of the 5th Infantry had clashed with Seminoles southeast of Lake Okeechobee. However, by the end of April 1857 Harney and the 5th Infantry had been transferred west to deal with uprisings in Kansas Territory, where hostility between abolitionist "jayhawkers" and pro-slavery "bushwhackers" was degenerating into something approaching outright guerrilla warfare.

A veteran of the Second Seminole War, Col Gustavus Loomis, replaced Harney as commander in Florida, but the withdrawal of the 5th Infantry left him with only ten companies of the 4th Artillery, which was later reduced to just four companies. Loomis organized volunteers into boat companies, which were given metal "alligator boats" built earlier specifically for use in the Big Cypress Swamp and Everglades. Measuring 30ft long, pointed at both ends, and drawing 2–3ft of water, each could carry up to 16 men into the swamps. While serving as a member of a boat company under Capt Jacob Mickler on the Kissimmee River during this period, Andrew Canova recalled seeing alligators "equal to trees in size, and vicious as wolves."

In November 1857 another boat patrol managed to capture 18 Seminole women and children from Billy Bowlegs' band; they also found and destroyed several villages and fields of crops. Probing into the Big Cypress Swamp on New Year's Day 1858, another amphibious expedition located and destroyed several Seminole towns and cultivated fields. Shortly after this, Loomis halted operations while a Seminole delegation from Indian Territory attempted to contact Bowlegs in order to persuade him to finally surrender. Having been granted their own reservation in Indian Territory separate from the Creeks, plus the offer of cash payments of $500 to each warrior and $100 to each woman, the renegade Seminoles at last agreed to stop fighting and go west.

On March 15, 1858, the bands led by Billy Bowlegs and Assinwar accepted the offer. On May 4 a total of 163 Seminoles were shipped to New Orleans, and four days later Col Loomis declared the war to be over.

AFTERMATH

Only about 100 Seminoles remained in Florida when the Third Seminole War finally ground to a halt. In December 1858 another attempt was made to remove those who remained, and two bands totaling 75 people came in and were transported to Indian Territory on February 15, 1859. This left the band under Arpiucki living inland from Miami and Fort Lauderdale, in southeast Florida; Chipco's band north of Lake Okeechobee; and individual families scattered across the wetlands of southern Florida. Since the war was officially over and the remaining Seminoles were staying quiet, the regular US Army units were reassigned and the volunteers were sent home. All of the forts established for the Seminole wars were decommissioned and soon stripped of any usable material by settlers.

In 1862 the Confederate state authorities of Florida contacted Arpiucki with promises of aid in an attempt to keep the Seminoles neutral during the Civil War. Although the Confederacy failed to keep their promises, the Seminoles were not interested in fighting another war. The 1868 Florida Constitution gave them one seat in the senate and one seat in the house of representatives of the state legislature, but they did not fill the positions, which were removed from the statute books in the 1885 constitution.

In 1957, the Seminoles signed a constitution and corporate charter which gave them legal federal recognition as the Seminole Tribe of Florida. In 1980 they numbered about 1,000 people, living on the Brighton, Immokalee and Big Cypress reservations and along the Tamiami Trail. At the same date the Seminoles who had been removed to Indian Territory (Oklahoma) numbered about 8,000.

SEMINOLE DRESS

The tribes that became the Seminole confederation had already replaced much of their native clothing with that made from European trade goods by the commencement of the First Seminole War in 1818. Some took pride in wearing items of uniform captured from US soldiers. For example, after the battle of Withlacoochee in December 1835, members of the force under Gen Clinch observed that Osceola was "distinguished [seen] by several, having on a uniform coat of our army, occupying a conspicuous station, where he could observe the movements of the army." Troops in the column commanded by Gen Gaines during March 1836 observed several black Seminoles with "soldiers' clothing on." (When Coacoochee and his band surrendered they were reported to be dressed in colorful costumes they had stolen from a theatrical group.)

The 1857 volunteer Andrew P. Canova described the discovery of some Seminole clothing in an encampment discovered by troops in "alligator boats" during Harney's campaign of that year:

> Hanging in one of the wigwams [sic] were two chiefs' costumes, richly embroidered with beads. Some breast-plates [gorgets], hammered out of silver dollars, were also found. We made a dash for these, and I was fortunate to secure one of these costumes. This consisted of a sort of waistcoat, a pair of leggings and moccasins, and a sash. Each article was covered with elaborate designs, worked in beads and silk, representing birds, fishes, etc., and must have cost much time and patience.

Headdress

The very distinctive headdress of the Seminoles consisted of a turban with much plumage, encircled by a silver or white-metal headband. Chiefs were distinguished by ostrich-feather plumes. At a council meeting on November 10, 1840, a chief called Halleck wore "a fine turban ornamented with black ostrich feathers." According to a contemporary newspaper account published during his visit to Washington, DC, in 1853, Billy Bowlegs wore "a kind of turban enclosed in a broad silver band and surmounted by a profusion of black ostrich feathers." According to artist and soldier John Rogers Vinton,

> On occasions of ceremony … there are certain peculiarities of costume which are seldom departed from. For instance the ostrich plumes which decorate the heads of the Chiefs. These are worn differently by different individuals. Coa Harjo [Coeehájo] wore his on the front part of his head and so did most of the other chiefs I saw, with certain modifications – but Osceola was peculiar for wearing his always on the opposite side and hanging off to the rear…

Osceola may have worn his turban in this fashion to accommodate the distinctive hairstyle of Seminole men which was described by Clay MacCauley:

> The men cut all their hair close to the head, except a strip about an inch wide, running over the front of the

Painted by Charles Bird King c.1826, Micanopy led the Seminoles during the ambush and massacre of Dade's command in December 1835, and continued a fierce opposition to the American invasion of Florida until his surrender in May 1837. He is depicted wearing the typical headgear of a Seminole chief, consisting of a red turban topped by black ostrich feathers. The "long shirt" is shown as dark sky-blue, with red zigzag trim and white appliqué edging on the fringed cape. (Author's collection)

THE SEMINOLE AND THEIR ALLIES, 1817–19
1: Seminole chief
2: Black Seminole warrior
3: "Maroon" warrior

A

JACKSON'S ARMY, 1818–19
1: Private, 4th US Infantry
2: Georgia militiaman
3: Creek warrior

B

SEMINOLE WARRIORS, 1835–42
1: Seminole chief
2: Seminole warrior
3: Seminole warrior with US Army jacket

C

US ARMY, NAVY & MARINE CORPS, 1836–42

1: Private, 4th US Infantry

2: Private, US Marine Corps

3: Private, 1st Regiment of Dragoons

4: Able Seaman, US Navy

US MILITIA, 1836–42
 1: Irish Volunteers, South Carolina Inf Regt (Brisbane's)
 2: Edgefield Blues, Brisbane's Regiment
 3: Officer, Brisbane's Regiment

E

CAMPAIGN DRESS, 1856–57
1: US regular infantryman
2: Florida Volunteer
3: Seminole woman captive

F

US REGULARS, GARRISON DRESS, 1855–58
1: First Lieutenant, US Infantry
2: Musician, 5th US Infantry
3: Private, US Artillery in infantry service

G

SEMINOLE WARRIORS, 1857

1: Seminole chief
2: Black Seminole warrior
3: Seminole warrior in partial European dress

H

scalp from temple to temple, and another strip, of about the same width, perpendicular to the former, crossing the crown of the head to the nape of the neck. At each temple a heavy tuft is allowed to hang to the bottom of the lobe of the ear. The long hair of the strip crossing to the neck is generally gathered and braided into two ornamental queues [see Plate C3].

By the 1850s the shape of the turban had changed considerably; MacCauley described it as

a remarkable structure … made of one or more small shawls. These shawls are generally woolen and copied in figure and color from the plaid of some Scotch clan. They are so folded that they are about 3 inches wide and as long as the diagonal of the fabric. They are then, one or more of them successively, wrapped tightly around the head, the top of the head remaining bare; the last end of the last shawl is tucked skilfully and firmly away, without the use of pins, somewhere in the many folds of the turban. The structure when finished looks like a section of a decorated cylinder crowded down upon the man's head. I examined one of these turbans and found it rather a firm piece of work, made of several shawls wound into seven concentric rings. It was over 20 inches in diameter, the shell of the cylinder being perhaps 7 inches thick and 3in width. This headdress, at the southern settlements, is regularly worn in the camps and sometimes in the hunt.

Body garments

The everyday outer garment worn by the Seminoles was the knee-length "long shirt," with a caped collar and fringing. This might be made from either cloth or hide such as deerskin. The cloth version was usually made from patterned or embroidered calico with appliquéd cloth or beaded zigzag trim. Those made from hide were often embellished with colorful glass beadwork and embroidery. Underneath this was a shorter "plain shirt," which was copied from 18th century British shirts. This garment remained relatively unchanged throughout the period and could be cotton pinstripe, calico or gingham, with crimped edging to a beaded caped collar. The breech cloth worn by the Seminoles was of a tapered shape typical of all Southeast Native American cultures. Early 19th century Seminole breech cloths appear to have been decorated in the same style as the "long shirt," while later examples seem to have been plain or with more simple trim.

Legwear

The fabric used for leggings worn by the Seminoles was usually "strouding" – a wool broadcloth made in England and named for the mills at Stroud in Gloucestershire. Probably introduced by the English traders during the latter part of the 18th century, this was usually red, although blue may also have been used. Seminole chiefs were particularly partial to wearing red leggings. When artist George Catlin was commissioned by the US War Department to paint the

The chief Tokosee Mathla was also painted by Charles King Bird in 1826. The red turban has a scallop-edged silver band and black plumes. The "long shirt" appears to be striped in brown and dark blue, with white trim and fringing on the cape but red fringing on the edges of the skirt. The shawl around the neck, the waist sash and the front-buttoning leggings are scarlet. Note the silver armbands, and a peace medal from his visit to Washington, DC, hanging below the silver gorget. Osceola had Tokosee Mathla killed that same year, "by sending sixteen bullets through him," for supporting Seminole removal west. (Author's collection)

most prominent Seminole chiefs then in captivity at Fort Moultrie, South Carolina, Micanopy was approached first, but positively refused to be painted. After much persuasion he at last consented, saying,"If you make a fair likeness of my legs," which he had very tastefully dressed in a handsome pair of red leggings, "you may paint Micanopy for the Great Father."

In common with those of all Southeastern Native Americans, Seminole leggings might have either front or side seams, although the former was most common, and were fastened by brass buttons. Worn over the moccasins, they were edged with military trim or silk ribbon, and decorated with beadwork; this was generally restricted to zigzag patterns, unlike the more elaborate and colorful Creek designs. MacCauley observed "one pair of leggins made of a bright red flannel, and ornamented along the outer seams with a blue and white cross striped braid." Buckskin leggings were also commonly worn. According to Cory, the Seminole hunted wearing nothing but "a cotton shirt unless it is a very rough country, when he sometimes wears leggings made of soft leather." Unlike leggings of many other tribes, those worn by the Seminoles closely followed the contours of the leg and were almost skin-tight, being tied together with thongs. They were usually plain but often embellished with a fringed leather garter. Covering the leg from mid-thigh to ankle, they not only afforded protection from the hazards of Florida's vegetation but also from insect stings and bites. Seminole moccasins were plain leather and, according to MacCauley, were "… made of buckskin, of either a yellow or dark red color. They are made to lace high about the lower part of the leg, the lacing running from below the instep upward."

Decoration

As in most Native American cultures, face and body paint was particularly important to the Seminoles. Regarded as the color of war, red was painted in bands or stripes on the face, as well as on the backs of the hands and on knife-handles. Black was also worn on the face as part of the preparation for war. Some warriors entered battle naked except for a breech cloth with their bodies streaked in bizarre patterns with red and black paint. In 1842, Halleck Tustenuggee and his band attacked a company of the 2nd Dragoons in "a state of nudity, their bodies painted scarlet." Green worn under the eyes was supposed to empower the wearer with night vision. Considered the color of "old Bones," yellow paint indicated that a warrior was ready to die. White was the color of peace, and a strip of white worn around a Seminole turban indicated that the wearer was prepared for a truce. On occasions when Billy Bowleg wanted to parley he left a sign of white beads and tobacco leaves on the trail leading to his camp.

Silver or silver-gilt crescent-shaped gorgets were worn by officers in most European armies in the 18th and early 19th centuries, both as a badge of rank and an indication that they were on duty. In some cases Native American chiefs were awarded a military rank for service given to the British in time of war, in which case they were given an officer's gorget. As time passed the fashion spread among various Southeastern Native American cultures, including the Seminoles, who heated silver coins and pounded them together to reproduce the gorget shape. Some Seminole chiefs wore as many as four silver crescents suspended from

John Horse – also known as Juan Caballo, John Cowaya and Gopher John – was born in 1812 in Florida of a black mother and a Native American father. Described as 6ft tall and powerfully built, he was regarded as an expert marksman. A leader of black Seminoles, he served as an interpreter for a number of Seminole chiefs, and was involved in freeing 700 Native Americans and blacks from a relocation camp near Fort Brooke in June 1837. Captured that same year, he escaped with 17 other inmates from Fort Marion and fled to Okeechobee, where, in December, they fought the last major engagement of the Second Seminole War. John Horse was ultimately persuaded to surrender in the spring of 1838; after transportation to Indian Territory he served as an interpreter for the US Army and continued to campaign for Seminole/black rights. Afraid of being taken into slavery with the passage of the Fugitive Slave Law in 1850, he led many of the black Seminoles to the safety of Mexico, where many of his descendants live to this day. (*Origin, Progress, and Conclusion of the Florida War*, 1848)

their neck. Billy Bowlegs wore three, "to which was appended a large silver medal with … a likeness of President Van Buren … his throat was thickly covered with strands of large blue beads, and he also wore bracelets of silver over the sleeves of his decorated hunting shirt."

Equipment and weapons

The Seminoles almost invariably wore bandoliers which supported large pouches made from "strouding" or blanket cloth, with beaded tassels at both ends of the bandolier and along the bottom edge of the pouch. Decorated with colorful beadwork, these contained "powder, bullets, pocket knife, a piece of flint, a small quantity of paper, and like things for use in hunting," according to MacCauley. Bead-embroidered and tasselled waist sashes were also worn, and these often had side-arms such as knives or pistols tied into them.

The traditional weapons of the Seminoles included spears with flint, bone or cane tips, and war-clubs studded with shark's teeth, plus bows and arrows. However, after contact with European armies many Seminoles converted to modern weaponry and learned to use Spanish and American muskets and rifles to great effect. The "Kentucky" rifle was popular due to its economical use of lead and powder. American soldiers reported that their "sentinals on duty were wounded by single shots from the Seminole rifles at a distance of four or five hundred yards."

US UNIFORMS, WEAPONS & EQUIPAGE

Most enlisted US regulars were provided with the Army undress or fatigue uniform throughout the three main periods of warfare in Florida. As officers bought their own clothing, many wore whatever they pleased, and most chose not to wear full dress. As a result of supply difficulties, regular units based in Florida finally stopped receiving full dress uniform coats and caps soon after the beginning of the Second Seminole War.

US REGULAR TROOPS
1818–19

Those troops that did receive full dress during the First Seminole War wore a uniform prescribed on May 1, 1813. This introduced a plain dark blue uniform which brought an end to the last remnants of 18th-century colored cloth trimmings and facings on the soldier's coat. It consisted of a "plain blue coatee [tail-coat] … with white or buff cross belts, white vests and white overalls with black gaiters for Infantry and Artillery." The coats were to be "single breasted, to button from the collar to the waist." White tape edging and "blind" buttonholes embellished the collar of infantry, and the same in yellow for artillery.

This unidentified infantryman wears the sky-blue undress uniform trimmed with white, in use throughout the Second Seminole War; note the "blind buttonholes" on the stand collar extending right back to buttons below his ear, and the protruding handkerchief showing the position of the pocket. He holds an M1840 non-commissioned officer's sword. Note that this image is reversed left-to-right. (Courtesy of William Schultz, MD)

White cotton drill uniforms were supplied to all three US Army regular branches of service (infantry, artillery and dragoons) during the Second Seminole War. The white metal "eagle" buttons and the epaulettes on this "roundabout" jacket indicate that it was worn by an infantry officer. (Courtesy of www.historicalimagebank.com)

The new 1813-pattern headgear adopted was made of leather instead of felt but was otherwise modelled on the British 1812 or "Belgic" shako. Cylindrical in shape, it was nicknamed the "tombstone cap" for the high false front piece rising above the crown by approximately 3 inches. By the beginning of the First Seminole War this feature had white trim or paint on its edges. Rectangular white metal cap plates for infantry were not always present, but bore an eagle, flag and drum motif, with "INFANTRY" above and "[number] REGT" below. That for artillery was brass, and showed an unfurled flag with staff, cannon and stack of cannon balls, with "ARTILLERY" above and "[number] REGT" below. These caps had a white worsted plume secured in a long leather socket on the left side with a black leather cockade at its base, and a tasselled white cord was secured diagonally from top right to bottom left. A separate piece of thin leather was attached at the back to afford additional protection from the weather, and could be buttoned up when not in use. Inside, a strip of sheepskin served as a sweatband, and there was also a bag-like linen lining with drawstring.

Field officers also wore dark blue tail-coats and were distinguished by silver epaulettes and a red waist sash. Their headgear was a black bicorn hat with gold pull-cord tassels, white plume, and cockade and button. White pantaloons were tucked into black leather Hessian boots.

The undress or fatigue uniform worn by the infantry and artillery during the First Seminole War consisted of a "sleeved jacket" or "roundabout," described as being of "very dark mixed gray," with a nine-button front fastened by pewter "US" buttons, shoulder straps, and a 4in standing collar. Pockets on each side of the lower breast had welted or reinforced tops. A thick black glazed-leather stock was worn around the neck. Trousers were plain white hemp twill "Russia" sheeting overalls, with a front seam and small front flap, plus 2in slits let into the cuffs, which were cut only to the ankle. Worn under the overalls and strapped under the arch of the foot, half-gaiters of black wool came to just below the knee and were fastened at the side with 15 small pewter uniform buttons. Footwear consisted of black leather low-quarter shoes with two or three laceholes.

The main weapon carried by US infantry in the First Seminole War was the M1795 contract flintlock musket. Commonly called the "Springfield musket," this had been the standard long arm during the 1812–15 war, and was derived from the French M1763 "Charleville" flintlock supplied during the Revolutionary War. It is estimated that by 1814 about 30,000 M1795 muskets were being produced annually, and many of these remained in service in 1817, despite the introduction of the M1809 and 1812 contract muskets. The latter did not reach the production stage until 1815.

Accoutrements consisted of the 1808-pattern cartridge box slung over the left shoulder on a 2¼in-wide crossbelt and carried on the right hip. The bottom half of this box accommodated a tin insert for carrying gun flints, and was accessible through a small flap on the pouch front. Above this was a wooden block bored to accommodate 26 paper cartridges. The removable sling was fastened to square steel buckles on the bottom of the box. This type of cartridge box was widely contracted by a variety of makers and was in general use until 1836. A black leather bayonet scabbard was carried on a crossbelt over the right shoulder and rested on the left hip. The bayonet belt had an oval-shaped white metal 1815-pattern plate bearing an eagle, flag and drum motif. Also suspended over the right shoulder was a black-painted linen haversack. The canteen was of the wooden barrel type and painted light Prussian blue, with the regimental number painted as an elaborate red script numeral; it was carried on an inch-wide black leather sling. Knapsacks carried included the Lherbette 1808 patent model made of heavy canvas and painted light Prussian blue, with a red "U.S." inside a white oval, and also the hard wooden-framed, canvas-covered box pattern.

1835–42

A militia officer described a company of regular infantry on campaign in Florida in May 1836: "Here was a company drawn up, which could scarcely be distinguished by any uniform, except that of dirt, from the common militia: [but] their upright heads, and close touching elbows showed that they were regulars; their blue suits were bemired out of recollection, and their brightened belts were now tarnished …".

Of the Dade massacre of December 1835, George A. McCall recalled "The picture of those brave men lying thus in their 'sky-blue' clothing, which had scarcely faded, was such as can never be effaced from my memory."

Headgear for all regulars during the Second Seminole War was either the 1825-pattern shako or the 1833-pattern folding leather forage cap. The former was a "wheel" cap of dark blue wool, the crown of which was

Introduced in 1820 and worn by the US Army until at least 1839, this greatcoat button displays the letters "U.S." with a spread eagle above and an oval wreath below. The reverse, with a bent-over shank, shows the back mark "*** UNITED *** STATES". This was dug up at Fort Brooke between 1974 and 1988. (Author's collection)

This one-piece gilt metal button dug up on the site of Fort Brooke bears an eagle, with a shield to the right, on a lined field. It has been identified as a militia button; some 1839-pattern cap chinstraps also appear to have been secured by buttons of this design. (Author's collection)

framed in white and decorated with 20 "spokes" of black worsted cord radiating out from a white metal button in the center. This cap was finished with white branch-of-service trim around the band for infantry and yellow for artillery, and had a wide brim of black leather called a "poke."

Each man was issued with one forage cap for every five-year enlistment. The 1825-pattern cap saw continued service into the late 1830s, despite the fact that it offered little protection in foul weather. Designed to overcome this problem, the 1833-pattern cap was made of goatskin (except those supplied to the West Point cadets, which were morocco leather.) Sometimes known as the "gig top," it consisted of a tall, collapsible soft leather cap with patent leather visor and chin strap. First issued to the newly established Regiment of Dragoons, the version worn by that unit had a small flap in the rear which could be unbuttoned and unfolded to a depth of 6in to protect the back of the neck from the elements. For insignia on this cap the infantry wore a white metal company letter, the artillery and dragoons yellow metal letters. Among those contracted to produce this headgear was James M. Hill, a hatter at Blackhorse Alley, Philadelphia, who supplied 3,000 infantry and artillery forage caps and 500 dragoon forage caps in 1836. Of its use in Florida, a hospital steward commented that at night it was worn with the chin strap buckled under the chin in order to "keep out of our ears ear-wigs, centipedes, cockroaches, etc."

Undress or fatigue jackets consisted of sky-blue kersey "roundabouts" with white trim for infantry and yellow for artillery and dragoons around all edges of the high collar, plus two long blind buttonholes (tape loops) terminating at the rear in small buttons. Shoulder straps were also edged according to branch-of-service color. The jacket was fastened with nine large two-piece, convex white metal infantry "I" buttons, plus one button of the same size on each cuff closure. As with jackets worn in the First Seminole War, this garment had pockets on each side of the lower breast with welted or reinforced tops. Trousers were also of sky-blue kersey, with a fall front fastened with plain white metal buttons and without pockets. A cord tie at the rear adjusted the waist size.

All three branches of service were issued a plain white cotton drill "roundabout" for warm weather duty. This was of the same pattern as the sky-blue jacket but without the collar and shoulder-strap trim. It had the same number of buttons down the front, with white metal "eagle I" buttons for infantry, and yellow metal "eagle A" and "eagle D" for artillery and dragoons respectively. White cotton pantaloons were of the same pattern as the blue version, with a fall front and cord size-adjustment at the rear. Footwear was 1822-pattern black leather lace-up boots.

These uniforms were worn day and night and soon became ragged and dirty. Likewise, all of the white leather belting was blackened, and metal items such as cap numbers and buttons were either removed or allowed to tarnish in order to make the wearer inconspicuous to Seminole marksmen. According to Coacoochee, during the Second Seminole War many of the Seminoles mocked the US regulars "floundering with their arms and accoutrements in mud and water" through the swampland in pursuit of their quarry.

Regarding weapons and accoutrements, the infantryman carried the M1816 .69cal smoothbore flintlock musket with 18in bayonet. Although the 1828-pattern cartridge box with decoratively embossed "eagle" flap saw some service, it was discontinued in favor of what would become the plain-flapped 1839 pattern. These boxes were carried on a crossbelt (originally whitened buff leather, later blackened), with a pick-and-brush set attached to the coat. Bayonets were suspended from an 1828-pattern leather crossbelt with a white metal oval 1815-pattern plate. Haversacks were of white cotton and fastened by three buttons. Suspended from russet leather slings, canteens were still of the model used during the First Seminole War, painted Prussian blue and marked with the regimental number and company letter.

In order to be less distinguishable in the field, officers tended to wear unostentatious clothing to blend in with their men, and their side-arms and accoutrements were also modified considerably to suit the extreme conditions in Florida. In 1841, Capt George A. McCall of the 4th US Infantry wrote: "On all these marches, I carried my seven days' rations in a bag rolled in my blanket and strapped across my shoulders, together with an extra flannel shirt (the only wear on such tramps) and pair of socks, besides my double gun – swords being worse than useless." An officer commanding a group of about 40 scouts in US service, who looked more like "banditti than a body of soldiers," was described by Capt John T. Sprague, 8th US Infantry, as being "without shoes or stockings, his pantaloons sustained by a belt, in which were thrust a brace of pistols, without vest or coat, his cap with a leathern flap behind, to divert the rain from coursing down his back; in this manner he led his detachment through bog and water, day after day; dependent for food upon the contents of his haversack strapped to his back."

1855–58

The uniforms worn by the regulars who fought the Third Seminole War were patterned on the Regulations of 1851. Inspired by French military fashion, these superseded the marked British influence that had flavored the dress of the American army since the Colonial era.

Headgear consisted of a tall, slightly tapering dark blue cloth-covered cap which, since January 1854, had a welt of branch-of-service color around the band: sky-blue for infantry, scarlet for artillery, emerald-green for riflemen, orange for dragoons, yellow for engineers, and crimson for the ordnance department. Serving for fatigue wear as well as full dress from 1855, in its latter use this cap was surmounted by a round worsted pompon of corresponding branch color. When the cap was worn for garrison duty or field service the pompon, insignia and stiffening were removed so that the sides collapsed and the top tended to incline forward. The wide-crowned 1839-pattern forage cap was also commonly still worn for campaign and fatigue duty.

The 1851-pattern nine-button dark blue frock coat worn by enlisted men by 1857 had branch-color trim around the collar and cuffs. That worn by officers was slightly longer and lacked the colored trim, having false pockets in the rear skirts. A "chasseur-à-pied" pattern coat with pleated skirts was adopted in 1855, but saw only limited service through 1857. Trousers were sky-blue cloth for both regimental officers and men, and dark blue for all other officers. Those worn by general officers were plain; regimental officers and all enlisted men had an $1/_8$in seam stripe in branch-of-service color.

Both of these one-piece buttons were dug at the site of Fort Brooke, and are associated with the establishment of that post in 1824. The smaller cuff-sized example displays a spread eagle above a cannon with a stack of six cannonballs below the muzzle, above "CORPS"; this design was worn by the Artillery Corps of the US Army during the 1814–1825 period. The larger coat button, produced after the re-organization of the US Army in 1821, was worn by a member of the Light Artillery, 1st Regiment; it bears the script letters "LA" encircled by 16 five-pointed stars on a lined field. (Author's collection)

Although the 1851-pattern dress cap with the stiffening removed was being worn for fatigue purposes by the mid-1850s, the flat-crowned 1839-pattern cap was also still in widespread use. This example was worn by Capt James Duncan, Company A, 2nd Artillery. (West Point Museum Collections, United States Military Academy)

The main weapon carried by both infantry and artillery serving as infantry in Florida from 1855 through 1858 was the US M1842 .69cal smoothbore percussion-lock musket, some of which had been rifled and equipped with long-range sights since 1856. In use at the same time was the M1841 .54cal rifle, also known as the "Mississippi" or "Jaeger" rifle; since 1855 some of these had been re-rifled to .58cal, equipped with long-range sights, and provided with bayonet attachments and saber bayonets. Also available for issue were the M1855 .58cal rifle musket and rifle, both of which were fitted with the Maynard tape-primer magazine rather than using individual copper percussion caps.

Accoutrements included a cartridge box and cap pouch. The former was the 1839-pattern box with an oval brass "US" plate on the outer flap, which was designed to be carried on a crossbelt. Two internal tin containers arranged side by side each held ten rounds vertically on top, with a paper-wrapped package of another ten cartridges below. A small pouch was attached on the inside front beneath the flap, in which the soldier carried rifle tools, cleaning patches, and an oil rag. The other main cartridge box used during this period was designed for use with the M1841 rifle and had vertical loops for carriage on the waist belt; this type had a slightly smaller oval plate on the outer flap, and a single tin container inside.

Essential for carrying percussion caps, cap pouches used during the period 1855 through 1858 were the patterns of 1845 and 1850. Made of black bridle leather, the former was occasionally stamped with "US," had double flaps, and was lined with sheepskin to prevent the loose caps moving around and falling out. The outer flap engaged a brass stud on the front of the pouch. The 1850 type was the same except that the outer flap was longer and the brass stud was attached to the bottom of the pouch.

US VOLUNTEERS & MILITIA
1818–19

The volunteers and militia of Georgia, Kentucky, and Tennessee who fought in the First Seminole War were generally expected to provide most of their own clothing, weapons and equipment, so their appearance could hardly be described as uniform. Infantry and mounted riflemen mostly wore coarse linen or cotton hunting shirts and trousers of blue, black or gray. The hunting shirt was a thigh-length and single- or double-layered coat with an integral cape that provided additional warmth and protection for the shoulders; sewn back from the edge of the cut cloth, the seams often unravelled to produce a fringe. This was usually worn over a civilian shirt with long tails, capable of serving as camp- or night-wear. Tanned hide leggings were worn over fall-front trousers. Headgear consisted of a mixture of animal-skin caps, known as "mocknuters" and made from muskrat, rabbit and fox, with civilian beaverskin or felt round hats. Footwear generally consisted of sturdy, high-topped farmers' work shoes.

Accoutrements included broad brown leather waist belts with large brass frame buckles; leather pouches for carrying lead ball, extra rifle flints, and eating utensils; and powder horns. Canteens were usually of the unpainted wooden keg type suspended from a narrow cloth strap.

Weapons consisted of whatever men could provide: some carried the French .69cal Charleville musket without sling, others antiquated *escopetas* or Spanish carbines with distinctive "Catalan" stocks. Hunting knives and tomahawks were also carried as side-arms.

1835–42

The volunteers and militia who participated in the Second Seminole War came from Georgia, Alabama, Louisiana, South Carolina, Tennessee, Missouri, New York, Pennsylvania, and the District of Columbia. A few company-sized units provided themselves with campaign uniforms, while others wore their elaborate volunteer militia uniforms into US service. For example, one of three volunteer militia companies organized for one month's service during January 1836 to defend St Augustine, Florida, was the German Fusiliers, of Charleston, South Carolina. Their full dress consisted of

> a dark blue single-breasted coat, with cuffs … of red cassimere. The cuffs and collars were trimmed with Prussian binding and gold lace. On each side of the collar was a star of black surmounted by a gold cord, and each member wore a pair of red worsted epaulets. There were three rows of ball buttons on the front of the coat, eighteen buttons in each row. The skirts were trimmed with six ball buttons and were turned up and faced with white cassimere, having at the extremities two diamonds of red cloth. The pants were blue with three red stripes running down the side seams. Black stocks, white cross belts and waist belts, and a black military cap, surmounted by a plume of black and red feathers, completed one of the handsomest militia uniforms in the State.

Serving later in 1836 with the South Carolina Infantry Regiment commanded by Col Abbot H. Brisbane, the Irish Volunteers, also of Charleston, wore dark gray or drab "close-bodied short coats lined with their favorite green," pantaloons of the same hue with broad green seam stripes, and fur caps. Attached to the same regiment was the Edgefield Blues, who wore a "uniform dress of plain dark blue cloth coatees, ornamented with a few brass buttons on the skirts and sleeves, and trowsers that corresponded." According to one of its lieutenants, certain officers of this regiment wore full dress uniforms. Some of them:

> retained the silver winged, dock-tailed, stiff militia uniform coat; others rivalled the more handsome livery of United States officers, and shone conspicuous in golden epaulettes and superfine blue broad cloth; while others merely added the necessary accoutrements of an officer, such as sword, belt, and sash, to their plain but soldier-like suits of fustian; all had fatigue dresses calculated to withstand the wear and tear of marching and camping, for convenience and protection from the weather, and to supply the place of epauletted dress uniforms in encounters with the Indians, which were both unfit to charge through

Lt Isaac Bowen, 1st Artillery, saw service in Florida during the Third Seminole War. Photographed with a companion in the mid 1850s, he wears an 1839-pattern cap, and a frock coat with collar unhooked and turned down, beneath a civilian overcoat. The numeral "1" is embroidered in the center of his crossed-cannon cap insignia. (USAMHI/photo by Jim Enos)

hammocks with, and presented too conspicuous and enticing a mark for the rifle of the enemy. In these there was a singular variety. The water proof Caoutchouc [rubber] of dingy hue and buckram starchness, contrasted with the soft green and motley colored blanket coats; some wore the simple military round jacket, and some the easy backwoodsman's hunting shirt, while others were content with less military looking citizen's long tail blues, that had seen just service enough to recommend them for a campaign.

Colonel Goodwyn's Regiment of South Carolina Mounted Volunteers included a company of dragoons who were depicted in several lithographs produced in 1836–37 by Gray & James, wearing plumed 1833-pattern leather caps and red hunting frocks.

Although some clung to their unsuitable finery, most volunteers and militia wore hunting shirts and other forms of civilian clothing similar to that worn by the volunteers of 1818–1819. During early preparations for possible attack in 1836, many of the citizens of St Augustine paraded with "military buttons in their hats, to supply the want of uniforms." M. Myer Cohen noted that the militia of St Augustine paraded with cockades affixed to their hats. Surgeon's Steward John Bemrose, of the 2nd US Artillery, observed that the Florida Mounted Volunteers of 1835–36 wore plain "planter's dress" with the swords of the officers alone distinguishing them from their men. Consisting of two companies of infantry, the Tuscaloosa Volunteers, who served with Col William Chisolm's Alabama Regiment in 1836, were provided with "handsome" uniforms of unknown description made by local women before deployment to Florida.

Although largely dressed in civilian clothing, this young militia officer of the Third Seminole War period wears an 1839-pattern cap and 1834-pattern two-piece belt plate. (Author's collection)

Other units provided themselves with plain campaign dress, sometimes of coarse, ready-made "laborer's clothing" such as that marketed for use by slaves in the South. Among the units thus outfitted was Col Persifor Smith's Regiment of Louisiana Volunteers, who were provided with gray suits, and otherwise completely outfitted by the city of New Orleans. The Augusta Battalion, commanded by Maj Robertson, and Maj Mark A. Cooper's 1st Georgia Battalion of Foot, plus some companies of Georgia mounted volunteers, were also outfitted with coarse laborer's clothing by the state of Georgia in early 1836. Passing through Cherokee in August 1836, a company of Georgia mounted volunteers were described as having

their coats off with their muskets and cartouche boxes strung across their shoulders. Some of the men had straw hats, some of them with white felt hats, others had old black hats on with the rim torn off, and all of them were as unshaven and as dirty as they could well be. The officers were only distinguished by having Cherokee fringed hunting shirts on. Many of the men were stout young fellows, and they rode on, talking, and cursing and swearing, without any kind of discipline.

During the 1820s and 1830s the bulk of the weapons produced by the US government were distributed to the various states based on the returns of the strength of their militias. Since they served as US volunteer troops the majority of militia units participating in the Second

Serving in the 1st Regiment of Florida Mounted Volunteers during the Third Seminole War, Capt Winston Stephens wears civilian clothing including a checkered vest. He holds a US Army issue M1841 rifle with a sling; his waist belt – supporting a revolver holstered butt-forwards – and his slung powder horn appear to be of civilian origin. (Florida State Archives)

Seminole War were consequently equipped with these arms and accoutrements. The South Carolina militia companies which travelled to St Augustine in early 1836 did so equipped with state arms and accoutrements. General Winfield Scott drew weapons from several of these arsenals in early 1836, including those at Augusta, Georgia, and Mount Vernon, Alabama, and Gen Gaines drew arms from the Baton Rouge Arsenal to equip Persifor Smith's Louisiana Regiment. The large majority of these stockpiled US arms were most likely of War of 1812 vintage or earlier, such as M1795, 1809 and 1812 contract muskets. As the militia of the Territory of Florida was in an unorganized state when the war began in 1835, Gen Call purchased a large number of shotguns to equip the Florida mounted volunteers who subsequently took part in the first campaign of the war.

With regard to accoutrements and equipage, the law permitting War of 1812 volunteers to be issued with US Army tents, knapsacks, haversacks, canteens, and other camp equipage had been allowed to lapse by 1835. However, complaints from Scott brought swift action, and by March 1836 he was authorized to procure the necessary equipage for the volunteers who were being organized for Florida service. Unfortunately US arsenals did not have any great quantities of these necessary items on hand, and some volunteer units procured blankets and haversacks locally. It was not until the summer of 1836 that the shortage of equipment was resolved. Thereafter, volunteer units in Florida appear to have been completely outfitted with necessary accoutrements plus equipage, such as canteens, haversacks, knapsacks, tents, camp kettles, mess pans, spades, axes and hatchets.

1856–58

The first Florida volunteers mustered into Federal service at Fort Brooke in January 1856 were described as "124 men armed with rifles, double barrel guns, and mounted on horses and mules." According to an eye-witness, they rode without order through Tampa to the Federal garrison, most bearing their own arms which included "shot guns[,] muskets[,] double barrel fowling pieces … and everything else in the shape of firearms almost." Another account stated:

> Just imagine if you please that you see 124 men dressed in common material of various colors and ages, long beards and smooth chins … armed with every variety of blunderbusses[,] mounted on any sort of a horse from a poor pony to the large old rip – a few on mules and a few riding to one side, and you will have a correct view of the picture presented as they travelled the streets of Tampa helter skelter – without any order whatever.

By the time units of Florida Mounted Volunteers engaged in skirmishes with Seminoles in mid-1856 some were in receipt of US military arms. During a clash on the banks of the Peace River near Fort Meade on June 14, 1856, a detachment of volunteers from the companies of Capts Leroy Lesley and Francis Durrance charged into a Seminole camp, of which occasion one man recalled, "the peace and quiet … was disturbed by the vigorous clanking of US yagers [M1841 "Jaeger" rifles] discharged at the [Seminole] sentry as he went bounding through the swamp, hurly burly, pell mell." On being mustered for six months' service in

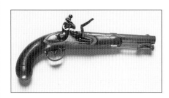

Some US troops serving in the Second Seminole War were armed with M1838 flintlock pistols; this example was manufactured for the Federal government by I.N. Johnson at Middleton, Connecticut. (Author's collection)

September 1857 the company commanded by Capt Robert Bullock were issued with 65 each of cartridge boxes and waist belts with plates, as well as a comprehensive collection of gun tools consisting of screwdrivers, wipers, cone picks, spring vices and bullet molds.

SELECT BIBLIOGRAPHY

Bazelon, Bruce S. & William F. McGuinn, *A Directory of American Military Goods Dealers & Makers 1785 –1885* (Manassas, VA; REF Typesetting & Publishing Inc, 1987)

Canova, Andrew P., *Life and Adventures in South Florida* (Tampa, FL; Tribune Printing Co, 1906)

Covington, James W., *The Billy Bowlegs War* (Chuluota, FL; The Mickler House Publishers, 1982)

Elwell, Rich, "Georgia Militia at Fort Cooper in the Second Seminole War" in *The Rebel Sabretache*, Vol. XIV: No.5, Atlanta Soldier Society (Sept–Oct 1988)

Giddings, Joshua R., *The Exiles of Florida & the War for Slavery* (New York, NY; Follett, Foster & Company, 1863)

Gilbert, Ed, *Frontier Militiaman in the War of 1812* (Oxford; Warrior 129, Osprey Publishing, 2008)

Goggin, John M., "Osceola: Portraits, Features, and Dress" in *The Florida Historical Quarterly*, Vol. XXXIII, Nos.3 & 9 (Gainesville, FL; 1955)

Hickox, Ron G., *US Military Edged Weapons of the Second Seminole War: 1835–1842* (Tampa, FL; R.G. Hickox, 1984)

Kochan, James L., *The United States Army, 1812–15* (Oxford; Men-at-Arms 345, Osprey Publishing, 2000)

Laumer, Frank, *Dade's Last Command* (Gainesville, FL; University Press of Florida, 1995)

MacCauley, Clay, "*The Seminole Indians of Florida*", Fifth Annual Report of the Bureau of Ethnology (Washington, DC; 1887)

Mahon, John K., *History of the Second Seminole War, 1835–1842* (Gainesville, FL; University of Florida Press, 1967)

Marshall, James E., "Arms and Accouterments of the Florida Mounted Volunteers in the 3d Seminole War, 1855–58" in *Military Collector & Historian*, Vol.60, No.2 (Summer 2008)

McBarron, H. Charles Jr, "4th US Infantry in the Seminole War, 1835–1842" in *Military Collector & Historian*, Vol.6, No.3 (September 1954)

McBarron, H. Charles Jr, "Colonel Brisbane's Regiment, South Carolina Militia, 1836" in *Military Collector & Historian*, Vol. 9, No.2 (Summer 1957)

McCall, George A., *Letters from the Frontiers* (Philadelphia, PA; J. B. Lippincott & Co, 1868)

Moore-Willson, Minnie, *The Seminoles of Florida* (New York, NY; Moffat, Yard & Company, 1914)

Porter, Kenneth W., "Billy Bowlegs (Holata Micco) in the Seminole Wars" in *Florida Historical Quarterly*, Vol.45 (1967)

Smith, William Wragg, *Sketch of the Seminole War & Sketches During a Campaign by a Lieutenant of the Left Wing* (Charleston, SC; Dan J. Dowling, 1836)

PLATE COMMENTARIES

A: THE SEMINOLE AND THEIR ALLIES, 1817–19

A1: Seminole chief
Based on contemporary portrait of Tukosee Mathla, alias John Hicks, this chief wears a red cotton turban topped with three black ostrich feathers and encircled by an ornate "German silver" headband. His fringed calico "long shirt" has a wide, caped collar and a knee-length skirt trimmed with embroidery and appliqué. A plain silver gorget is suspended around his neck, and he has German silver arm- and wrist-bands. His gaiter-style leggings are made from the English wool broadcloth known as "strouding", and are fastened with small brass buttons. His beaded knee garters are made of black strouding, and his shoes are plain buckskin moccasins. Essential to Seminole culture, his bandolier pouch is also of beaded and tasselled black strouding. He is armed with an antiquated Spanish *miquelet*-lock 7-bore flintlock hunting gun, with carved walnut stock and engraved barrel, and his accoutrements consist of a bullet pouch and powder horn.

A2: Black Seminole warrior
This figure is based on a contemporary engraving of John Horse, alias Gopher John. His blue turban is decorated with a plain German silver headband, plus two turkey feathers and a fantail of smaller eagle feathers at the rear. He wears a "plain shirt" of red strouding with crimped edging around its beaded collar. His dark blue beaded armbands are of the same type of cloth. He has buckskin leggings and moccasins, and beaded black knee garters. He brandishes a Spanish *miquelet* pistol, and has a hunting knife with German silver inlay in a leather sheath tied into his waist sash.

A3: "Maroon" warrior
This "maroon" or free black is armed with a British Army "Brown Bess" flintlock musket, and accoutrements consist of a crudely-stitched dark leather ball pouch and a scrimshawed powder horn. Suspended from his waist belt is a large knife with stag-antler grip. Seen in the background is the "Negro Fort" which served as a headquarters for Seminole and black resistance until its destruction in 1816.

B: JACKSON'S ARMY, 1818–19

B1: Private, 4th US Infantry
This regular soldier wears an 1813-pattern leather "tombstone" shako with a folding, buttoned rear neck flap. It bears a white metal 1815-pattern plate (see accompanying photo), and is dressed with a tasseled worsted cord running diagonally across the front, and a white worsted tuft above a circular cockade of embossed black leather with a small painted eagle encircled at its center. His "sleeved jacket" or "roundabout" has pewter "US" buttons, a 4in standing collar, reinforced pocket tops, and shoulder straps; note the leather stock around his neck. His hemp twill trousers or overalls have a small front flap or fall-front, with central seam. Immersed in swamp water, his black wool half-gaiters are fastened at the side with 15 small pewter buttons, and have linen straps passing under the arch of his black leather low-quarter shoes. He carries an M1795 Springfield musket with whitened buff leather sling. His accoutrements are an 1808-pattern cartridge box and a black scabbard encasing a socket bayonet with a 16in triangular-section blade, both of which are suspended from blackened leather cross belts, the bayonet belt with a white metal oval plate displaying the "eagle, drum and flag." In the field he is equipped with a black-painted linen haversack, a blue-painted wooden canteen, and an 1808-pattern Lherbette canvas knapsack suspended on H-straps.

B2: Georgia militiaman
He wears a black felt round hat with fore-and-aft peak and a black leather cockade bearing a small metal eagle badge. His drab-colored cloth hunting shirt with integral double cape shows an unravelled red cloth fringe. Tanned hide leggings cover his black cloth trousers. He is armed with a French .69cal Charleville musket, and his gear consists of a powder horn and leather ball pouch, an unpainted wooden canteen, and a hunting knife with a white bone grip tucked in his waist belt.

B3: Creek warrior
Dressed much like a Seminole, this American-allied warrior is based on a portrait of William McIntosh, the Creek (or Muskogee) chieftain (see page 7). His brown fur cap has a polished metal band and black fur "tail," and a tall red-tipped white ostrich feather. He wears a homespun "long shirt" with red edging and fringe, over a checked cotton shirt with yellow-lined collar and red fringed cuffs. Beaded leggings with knee garters cover his lower legs, and his bandolier belt and pouch are also heavily beaded. A red sash is wrapped around his waist, and he carries a US Mounted Artillery officer's saber with brass hilt and curved blade.

C: SEMINOLE WARRIORS, 1835–42

C1: Seminole chief
Based on a painting of Osceola (see page 18), this chief displays red half-face paint signifying war and destruction. His cotton turban is decorated with ostrich feathers and tied to the back of his head via his plaited scalp-lock; it covers his roach hairstyle, leaving only the front fringe and forelocks exposed. A beaded bandolier bag and red waist sash are worn over his patterned and fringed "long shirt". He wears necklaces of bead and shell, and three gorgets. Leggings of red strouding are trimmed light blue and fastened with small brass buttons at the front; these cover plain buckskin moccasins. Knee garters of black strouding have blue beading and yellow ties. He is armed with a US M1819 Hall percussion conversion rifle.

Modelled on the British M1812 or "Belgic" shako, the US 1813-pattern leather infantry dress cap was worn by regulars serving in the First Seminole War – see Plate B1. This infantry version has a white worsted plume; the white metal rectangular plate with clipped corners bears the "eagle, flag and drum" motif, with "INFANTRY" above and " [number] REGT" below. A flap at the rear could be lowered to protect the soldier's neck from the elements. (Courtesy of www.historicalimagebank.com)

C2: Seminole warrior

Note the roach hairstyle with front fringe, side locks and rear braids. The green paint under his eyes was believed to aid vision, especially in the dark. His cotton "plain shirt" is copied from 18th century British garments, and is decorated with appliqué work. He wears buckskin leggings with fringed knee garters. Armed with a tomahawk, he also has a captured sailor's knife with inlaid ivory handle tucked in his richly beaded and tasselled waist sash.

C3: Seminole warrior with US Army jacket

Typically, this warrior with a simpler roach hairstyle has stripped down to a breech cloth and has streaked his body with war paint. Over this he wears a captured US infantry jacket, and an 1832-pattern cartridge box holds loads for his M1795 Springfield musket.

D: US ARMY, NAVY & MARINE CORPS, 1836–42
D1: Private, 4th US Infantry

The campaign dress includes an 1833-pattern folding leather forage cap with a brass numeral "4" attached to the front. His sky-blue kersey jacket has infantry-white trim on the collar and shoulder straps, and white metal pewter "eagle" buttons with "I" in a shield. His fall-front trousers are without pockets. Footwear consists of 1822-pattern lace-up boots. He is armed with a .69cal US M1816 flintlock musket; cross belts with an 1826-pattern plate support an 1808-pattern cartridge box and bayonet scabbard. He has a white cotton haversack, and a metal-banded wooden canteen painted Prussian blue with regimental and company designation painted beneath the "U.S." cypher.

D2: Private, US Marine Corps

The campaign dress of the marine includes a plain dark blue fatigue cap with a wide, stiffened top. His gray jacket has yellow trim on the collar and shoulder straps and yellow metal "eagle on anchor" buttons. Trousers of the same color have a fall front, and his gaiters are of black-painted canvas. He too carries an M1816 flintlock. With the exception of the knapsack, his accoutrements and equipment are Army issue, all of which were returned to Army stores after the Florida campaign.

D3: Private, 1st Regiment of Dragoons

This dragoon in summer campaign dress wears an 1833-pattern leather forage cap with company letter attached. His white cotton jacket has yellow metal "eagle D" buttons, and his white cotton trousers have a fall front. He is armed with an M1833 dragoon saber with quill-back blade, and carries a .525cal Patterson-Colt revolving cylinder percussion carbine. Fifty of these weapons were received by this regiment in March 1838, and a platoon of sharpshooters was formed within the unit. Equipage includes an 1833/37-pattern white buff leather saber belt with plain brass rectangular plate, and a carbine sling.

D4: Able Seaman, US Navy

This sailor equipped for shore duty wears a natural straw "sennit" hat with black cloth-covered underside and rim and a black silk ribbon. His white frock has blue-and-white trim on the collar, bib and cuffs, and his white duck trousers have a fall front and wide-cut legs. A black cotton handkerchief is tied around his neck, and he wears high-cut "Kipskin" black leather shoes. He has withdrawn his sheathed M1826-pattern cutlass from its frog, and has an M1826 Navy flintlock pistol on his hook-fastened waist belt.

The 1828-pattern cartridge box, with its decoratively stamped outer flap and whitened buff leather shoulder sling, saw limited service during the Second Seminole War. It was discontinued because the varnish tended to hide the elaborate floral and patriotic design on the flap. (Courtesy of www.historicalimagebank.com)

E: US MILITIA, 1836–42
E1: Private, Irish Volunteers, South Carolina Infantry Regiment (Brisbane's)

This volunteer militia company's full dress tail-coat of dark gray has green linings and trim and yellow metal "palmetto" buttons. Fall-front trousers of the same color, with inch-wide green seam stripes, are tucked inside knee-high tan leather leggings fastened with 12 small pewter buttons up the outside. Known during the 1830s as a "mocknuter," his fur cap is of a type commonly worn by militia in Florida. He is armed with an M1795 Springfield musket; the 1808-pattern cartridge box hangs from a whitened buff leather cross belt but the bayonet belt is black leather. He has a haversack and a keg canteen.

E2: Private, Edgefield Blues, Brisbane's Regiment

This company wore a plain blue tail-coat with yellow metal buttons, and fall-front pants of the same color are tucked into leather leggings. As with the Irish Volunteer, his gray beaverskin hat has a pink-and-white rosette attached. His weapon and accoutrements are also the same, and he has a gray blanket roll supported by a leather shoulder strap.

E3: Officer, Brisbane's Regiment

The undress coat is as prescribed for US Army field grade officers in 1832, with additional trim on the collar and sleeves but minus the "wings." His 1821-pattern black leather bell-crowned shako has a white metal "eagle" plate in front, a white metal scale chinstrap, white worsted cord and tassel, a leather cockade and a plume. His plain white cotton trousers are turned up at the ankles to reveal high-cut ankle boots. His sword has a stirrup-shaped guard, and his sword belt an 1826-pattern militia officer's "eagle" plate. Equipped for active service, he has a black-painted linen haversack, a wooden barrel canteen and a Lherbette knapsack.

The ancient gateway to the city of St Augustine is seen in the background.

F: CAMPAIGN DRESS, 1856–57
F1: US regular infantryman

The cap is the 1839 pattern with neck flap. He wears a plaid civilian shirt with his sky-blue kersey trousers, which have a fly front. He is armed with an M1842 percussion musket; his accoutrements are an 1841-pattern cartridge box on a black leather cross belt with an 1826-pattern "eagle" plate, and an 1850-pattern percussion cap pouch on a waist belt with oval "US" plate. A Bowie knife with tortoise-shell grip and

German silver mountings is also attached to his belt by a leather sheath and frog.

F2: Florida Volunteer

His completely civilian clothing consists of a slouch hat, shirt and vest with fly-front trousers. He is armed to the teeth, with an M1855 .64cal Colt revolving rifle, a Colt third model Dragoon revolver in a belt holster, and a Bowie knife.

F3: Seminole woman captive

This woman captured from a Seminole village surprised by an American column wears a very full, floor-length skirt gathered at the waist, and a long-sleeved blouse with a short attached cape decorated with silver discs. She has numerous strings of glass necklace beads, and is barefooted. Her child wears a European-style vest over a "plain shirt."

Burning in the background is a Seminole *chickee* or temporary dwelling, with palmetto thatch over an open cypress-log frame; these were typical of the swampland camps to which the Seminole retreated under American pressure.

G: US REGULARS, GARRISON DRESS, 1855–58

G1: First lieutenant, US Infantry

The scarlet sash over his right shoulder identifies him as "officer of the day". His headgear is an unadorned 1839-pattern cap. Rank is indicated by epaulettes showing a brass crescent, $1/_8$in bullion fringing and a single silver bar on the gold strap. His sky-blue trousers have $1/_8$in-wide dark blue seam welts. An M1850 line officer's sword is supported by a belt fastened with an 1851-pattern "eagle" plate.

G2: Musician, 5th US Infantry

His 1854-pattern dress cap has sky-blue infantry trim, but the pompon, stiffening and ornamentation have been removed and it has been compressed to form a forage cap. His 1851-pattern frock coat has the musicians' "herring-bone" worsted tape in sky-blue branch-of-service color on the breast. His drum is suspended from a whitened buff leather sling with brass drumstick holder attached, and his waist belt is fastened with a yellow metal oval "US" plate.

G3: Private, US Artillery in infantry service

The majority of the regular "infantry" for Harney's campaign were in fact provided by the 1st, 3rd and 4th Artillery. This soldier also has a compressed 1854 cap, with the appropriate scarlet branch-of-service trim. His 1851 coat is trimmed on collar and cuff with scarlet, and his sky-blue kersey trousers have $1/_8$in scarlet seam welts. He is armed with an M1842 percussion-lock smoothbore musket. The 1839-pattern cartridge box is slung from a black bridle leather cross belt bearing a round "eagle" plate; the 1845-pattern percussion cap pouch has a "US" stamp; and the 1853-pattern black-painted canvas knapsack has black leather straps.

This daguerreotype of Holata Mico, or "Billy Bowlegs," was taken during the visit of the Seminole delegation to Washington, DC, in 1852; see also Plate H1. When he stayed at the American Hotel at the Federal capital he was checked in as "Mr. William B. Legs." He died of smallpox in 1864. (Smithsonian Institution, National Anthropological Archives. Neg. no. 42-913)

H: SEMINOLE WARRIORS, 1857

H1: Seminole chief

Based on portraits of Holata Mico, alias "Billy Bowlegs," he wears a red turban with a broad silver band and black ostrich feathers. Beaded bandolier pouches are worn over a fringed and patterned calico "long shirt", and beaded and woven garters adorn his red cloth leggings. Suspended around his neck are three silver gorgets and a peace medal. He is armed with an M1851 .36cal Colt Navy revolver carried in a leather belt holster.

H2: Black Seminole warrior

This figure, based on portraits of Abraham, wears a loosely wrapped red turban and plain calico "long shirt" with a broad fringed collar and cape. His sky-blue kersey trousers and black brogans are of US Army origin. He has also acquired an M1842 percussion musket, complete with an 1839-pattern cartridge box on a black leather waist belt with oval "US" plate, and an 1845-pattern cap pouch.

H3: Seminole warrior in partial European dress

Influenced by years of contact with white settlers, this warrior armed with bow and arrow has donned a Derby hat and wears a black vest over his plaid "plain shirt." He has fringed buckskin leggings and garters and plain moccasins. A quiver filled with arrows is slung behind his shoulder.

The black Seminole leader Abraham – see also Plate H2 – survived all US efforts to hunt him down during the Second Seminole War, and remained at large in the Everglades after 1842. During the delegation to Washington in 1852 he served as an interpreter for "Billy Bowlegs". Produced by N. Orr, this engraving was published in 1848. (*Origin, Progress, and Conclusion of the Florida War*, 1848)

INDEX

Figures in **bold** refer to illustrations.

Aden, capture of (1839–1840) 4
Adlercron, Col John 8
Afghan Wars (1838–1842) 4
Arcot 3
artillery 37–39, **H3** (32, 47)
  Madras Horse Artillery **10**
  'the gunroom crew' 5
Assaye, Battle of (1803) 4

Baird, Sir David 44
Bannatyne, Capt Robert **A3** (25, 42)
Batta, the 10
bazaar money 9–10
Bengal Army 4, 5
  artillery 38
  cavalry 24, 33–35, **37, F2** (30, 45)
  colours 36
  engineers 39
  European infantry 13, 14, 15, **16**, 16,
    E2 (29, 45)
  the Great Mutiny (1857) 12
  native infantry 17, 18–19, **19, 21,** 40, 41,
    C1 (27, 43), **E1** (29, 44–45)
  standards 37
Bhaksar, Battle of (1764) 4
bhisties (water-carriers) 39
Bhurtpore 4
Bombay Army 6
  artillery 38
  cavalry 35–37, **H1** (32, 46–47)
  engineers 39
  European infantry 13, 14, 15, 16
  the Great Mutiny (1857) 12
  native infantry 17, 21–23, 40, **E3** (29, 45)
  standards 37
brinjarries (grain merchants) 39
Burma Wars 4

Caillaud, Capt 14
Calcutta 4
  fall of (1756) 5
  Fort William **6**
Candeish Bheel Corps 23
Canning, Lord 12–13
Carnatic Battalions 20, 36, **B** (26, 43)
cavalry 23–37, **37, D** (28, 44), **F** (30, 45),
  H1 (32, 46–47)
China Wars 4
chronology 3–4
Circar Battalions 20, 36
Clive, Robert 3, 4, 5, 17
Coast Sepoys 20
colours 36
Compagnie des Indes 3
Contingent Forces, Bengal Native Infantry
  18–19
Coorg campaign (1834) 4
Coote, Sir Eyre **8**, 39
Cornwallis, Lord 4, 7, 8, 9, 10, 13, 43

dragoons 23
Dundas, Henry 8, 10

East India Company, armies of *see also* uniforms
  artillery 5, **10**, 37–39
  cavalry 23–37, **37**
  chronology 3–4
  colours 36
  engineers 39
  European infantry 13–16, **33**
  followers 39
  native infantry 17–23, **24, 34,** 36
  organization of 7–11
  payment 9–10

standards 35, 37
  weapons **10, 14, 38, A1** (25, 42)
engineers 39
European infantry 13–16, **33, E2** (29, 45),
  H2 (32, 47)

Fisher, Capt J. 18
followers 39
Foot Artillery 38
Fort William, Calcutta **6**
Frontier Brigade, Bengal Native Infantry 19

Gold, Capt Charles **18**
golundaz 38
Governor General's Bodyguard 33–34, **37,** 45
Grant, Capt Alexander 5, 14
Great Mutiny (1857) 4, 6, 11–13
Grenadiers 17, 22
Gurkha War (1814–1816) 4
Guzerat Irregular Horse 35
Guzerat Provincial Battalion 23
Gwalior campaign (1843) 4

Haidar Ali 4
Horse Artillery 38
hussars 23, 24, **D2** (28, 44)
Hyderabad Contingent Cavalry 33

India Act (1784) 4, 7
India House, London **8,** 9
Indian Army 6, 7, 8, **9,** 13, 17–23, **20, 24,**
  A1 (25, 42), **C1** (27, 43), **B** (26, 43),
  E (29, 45), **F2** (30, 45), **F3** (30, 45), **G** (31, 46)
  colours 36
  the Great Mutiny (1857) 4, 6, 11–13
  organization of 10–11
  The Sepoy Line, 1845: 40–41
infantry, European 13–16, **33, E2** (29, 45),
  H2 (32, 47)
infantry, native 17–23, **24, 34, E** (29, 44–45),
  G (31, 46)
  colours 36

Java Light Cavalry **F3** (30, 45)

Kilpatrick, Lt James 23

Lake, Gen Gerald 4, 39
Lally, Baron 4
lancers 35
lascars 37–38
Laswari, Battle of (1803) 4
Lawrence, LtCol Henry 19
Lawrence, Maj Stringer **7,** 14, 16
Light Cavalry, Bengal 33–35
Light Cavalry, Bombay 35
Local Infantry, Bengal native infantry 18–19
Lumley, Capt 18
Lumsden, Capt 19

Madras Army 4, 5, **7,** 8
  artillery 38, **38, H3** (32, 47)
  cavalry 23–24, 25, **37, D1** (28, 44)
  colours 36
  engineers 39
  European infantry 13–14, **14,** 15, 16,
    A2 (25, 42), **C2** (27, 43), **H2** (32, 47)
  native infantry 17, **18,** 20–21, **24, 34,**
    40, 41, **B** (26, 43), **G** (31, 46)
  standards 37
Mahratta Wars 4, 6, 8, **10,** 21
Marine Battalion, Native Infantry 21
mercenaries 13
Miners 39
'Mogul Horse' cavalry 24, 33
Murray, Col John 35

muskets **14, A1** (25, 42)
Mysore Wars 4, 6, 8, 21

native infantry 17–23, **24, 34, E** (29, 44–45),
  G (31, 46)
  colours 36

O'Brien, Maj Lucius 45

Pathan cavalry 33
Persia 4
pistols **10**
Plassey, Battle of (1757) 4, 7
Polier, Capt 14
Pondicherry 4
Poona Auxiliary Horse 35
Poona Irregular Horse 35
Punjab Irregular Force 19

Raffles, Sir Stamford 45
Reid, Lt Charles 18
revenue money 9
Royal Artillery 37–38

Salmond, Col James Hanson 7
Sappers 39
Sawunt Warree Local Corps 23
Scinde, conquest of (1843) 4
Scinde Irregular Horse 35
sepoys 6, 7, 8, **9,** 13, 17–23, **20, 24, 34,**
  C1 (27, 43), **E** (29, 45), **F2** (30, 45), **F3**
  (30, 45), **G** (31, 46)
  colours 36
  the Great Mutiny (1857) 4, 6, 11–13
  organization of 10–11
  The Sepoy Line, 1845: 40–41
Seringapatam 4, **14, 35**
Shipp, John **10, 16**
Shore, Sir John 8–9, 10
Sikh Wars 4, 19
sillidar system 34
South Mahratta Horse 35
standards 35, 37
Stockdale, W.F.L. 7
Suffren, Adm de 4
Suraja Dowla 4
syce (grass-cutters) 39

Tippoo Sahib 4, **35**
Topasses 6

uniforms **10, 16, 17**
  artillery 38, **H3** (32, 47)
  cavalry 24–25, 34–35, **35, 37, D** (28, 44),
    F (30, 45), **H1** (32, 46–47)
  engineers 39
  European infantry **14, 16,** 16, **A2** (25, 42),
    A3 (25, 42), **C2** (27, 43), **E2** (29, 45),
    H2 (32, 47)
  native infantry **18,** 18, 19, **19,** 20–21, **21,**
    22–23, **34, B** (26, 43), **C1** (27, 43), **E1**
    (29, 44–45), **E3** (29, 45), **G** (31, 46)
  Rifle companies 17
  Royal East India Company Volunteers **15**
Urquhart, Capt John 7

Victoria, Queen 12

Wandewash, Battle of (1760) 4
War of the Austrian Succession (1740–1748) 3
Watson, Adm Charles 4
weapons
  9pdr guns **38**
  muskets **14, A1** (25, 42)
  pistols **10**
Wellesley, Gen Sir Arthur 4